Joys and Sorrows of Living with Adult Autism

Big Bertha Evans

PublishAmerica
Baltimore

© 2007 by Big Bertha Evans.
All rights reserved. No part of this book may be reproduced, stored in a retrieval system or transmitted in any form or by any means without the prior written permission of the publishers, except by a reviewer who may quote brief passages in a review to be printed in a newspaper, magazine or journal.

First printing

ISBN: 1-4241-7013-3
PUBLISHED BY PUBLISHAMERICA, LLLP
www.publishamerica.com
Baltimore

Printed in the United States of America

This book is dedicated to my mother-in-law Betty Evans. She has cancer really bad and this book is about her son; Brian. I also want to dedicate this book to everyone who has to deal with any aspect of Adult Autism. I do not have any facts or figures about the Autism spectrum disorder but I do have practical advice that just might work for you too. I pray this book helps all who read it.

Acknowledgments

A huge Thank You goes to my dear sweet loving husband, Brian Evans. Without him there would be no Joys and Sorrows of living with Adult Autism! I would still be typing too! I chicken peck, not type. One day I was pecking away with him standing behind me getting all FLUSTERPATED! That's a word I made up! He said "Can I type?" It was driving him nuts that I was so slow. I said PLEASE! He typed for me from then on.

Brian also had to remember the awful things that happened to him. He answered tons of questions I had about how or what he felt during each situation.

I also thank God my heavenly Daddy for bringing these two broken beings into one! I couldn't ask for a better husband, we were made for each other. I look back on my horrible past and I can see how each turmoil molded me into who I am today. I get a few needs I have fulfilled by God. Brian would provide for my every need if he could but because of his autism he is not capable of some things. My emotional needs, being the spiritual leader and my protector; in fact Brian said if someone took me he wouldn't go after them, he would take off running the other way!! God is my protector; He created all things. You don't mess with a child of God. If you do I feel sorry for you. The wrath of my heavenly Daddy is unlike anything you could ever imagine. God is Awesome!!!

Introduction

Hi my name is Big Hearted Bertha! I have a story of my own but I want to write about being married to an Autistic man. Simply stated it's like being married to a two year old stuck in a man's body but not in every area. One example is when a two year old sees a person he likes, he runs up to them and gives them a hug! My husband is the same way! He doesn't even have to know the person. If he likes how they look he will run up to them and give them a hug. I have to do a lot of explaining to people when he does this.

We were at the checkout and Brian saw this mother and daughter he liked the looks of and bobbed off and hugged them both. They both stood there in the state of shock by the look on their face. They were probably thinking, What just happened to us? Do we know this guy? I was checking out and I hadn't paid yet. I was praying, Hurry up! I have to go explain Brian to these ladies. As soon as I got done paying, I ran over there and said, I'm sorry. I have no idea who you are. My husband must have thought he knew you. You see he is autistic and he is like a 2-year-old and loves to give people he likes hugs whether he knows them or not. Their countenance immediately changed from shock to, Oh, that's so sweet. Everybody needs hugs.

I have to watch and if the person has a funny look on their face I have to tell him NOT to hug that person again, they were uncomfortable. It's usually a woman because men throughout his life were nothing but mean and condescending to him. Men make him feel very uneasy. Because he is autistic he cannot reason out why it is not okay to hug people he likes. He doesn't realize being a grown man they may feel uncomfortable having him hug them. In his eyes its just being nice, he does not ever have improper thoughts or feelings. Many people understand after I talk to them, but there are a few who still prefer not to be hugged. Brian is learning who he can hug and who not to hug, he feels sad, rejected, hurt and depressed, when someone doesn't want a hug nevertheless he complies.

My wonderful husband's name is Brian Evans. I'm not a writer but I have been reading all I can on Autism and it's never about Adults except for Temple Grandin and she is nothing like my husband. They are exact opposites. If I write in circles forgive me!

I'm going to have to give a little about me in order to start this awesome record of being married to an Autistic man, so here it goes.

Everything bad you can imagine has happened to me as a little girl. I married the first man to ever show me attention when I went to College of the Ozarks When I was in my foster home from 7th grade till the day after my graduation!, I wasn't allowed to even have a boyfriend. I was not a Christian and my whole life sex equaled love. He gave me that attention. When he graduated two years later I quit college and moved in with him. I now know that's wrong. We were going to have a real wedding for his mother. She was very ill and only had 10% of her stomach left from ulcer operations. She called me one day crying and screaming in pain saying her husband (my future father in law) had her other arm slamming the door on it over and over. She was so scared, so I called 911 and an ambulance. I had him put in jail. Three days later she was found dead, face down in her driveway by my future husband's grandfather. His son was immediately let out of jail because I was scared of pressing charges. I thought I would be next.

Anyway, we eloped. Four years into that marriage I was saved! I asked the Lord into my heart and life. I've never been sorry. After I received Christ I wouldn't drink, gamble, or anything bad. My Heavenly Father changed my want to.

You see we would go to Tunica every Friday and Saturday. I was an alcoholic. At first my now ex-husband would hold me between his legs and pour beer down my throat till I would get drunk, then have me do awful things, and tell me about what I did the next morning. Then, he found out I liked anything strawberry. He would buy tons of anything strawberry. Then I would willingly get drunk. Alcoholism runs in my family but I hated the flavor of beer, I thought it was fizzy urine. So it just took finding what I liked and I was an alcoholic like my daddy was. After I was saved I wouldn't do any of that anymore.

I didn't ever want to be alone so I decided I wouldn't get a divorce. I knew even before I got saved that it was wrong to get a divorce, but I told the Lord that I would show Christ in my life for one year and if he didn't change I would get one. I knew it couldn't be the Lord's will for his little girl to live like that. He did not change so I got one.

Courting

I met a pastor of a church in Berryville while working in receiving at Wal-Mart in Harrison he had invited me to hear him preach. So I did every Wednesday and twice on Sunday.

I quit Wal-Mart and opened my own housekeeping business, B & B Housekeeping.

While I was going to the church in Berryville this really handsome young man would come every now and then and sing a song at church before the pastor would preach. Boy! oh boy!, could he ever sing. He would bellow his song from his heart so beautifully! I remember thinking wouldn't it be nice to have a man like that to serenade you! Little did I know I would marry that handsome young man a few years down the road. I got saved on my birthday, September 4, 1997! November 20, 1998, two months after my divorce I had a near fatal accident. That story is a book all its own, so I won't elaborate except to tell you that after my divorce I decided I would never give another man the time. I was stuck on me. Nobody would ever be good enough. God had to practically kill me in order to humble me for the most wonderful man ever Brian!

The first time he saw me he thought I was married, (I was) the second time he thought I had a boyfriend, (I did) the third time he couldn't get enough nerve to ask me himself, so he asked someone else to who did not ask me. (I would have had to break his heart).

The pastor told me to focus on getting better for 1 year after my wreck before I could think about boys. I was living in the parsonage garage apartment. It had only been 9 months, so I would have had to say no. The next time he finally got the nerve to ask me out on a date. I said yes!

Brian and his mother came to visit all his aunts, uncles, and cousins who lived in Berryville. That's why he would show up every now and then. Brian would pick me up at 7:30 am in the morning and have me home by 10:00 pm. I had so much fun! This man just adored me all the time. We talked about my past, his past, everything. We had so much in common. We both had brain damage, we loved the out doors. We also loved games and walking trails. We would go walk on top of this mountain covered with trees. It was so beautiful to see and appreciate God's glory with a man who just oozed with loving affection! This affection for the first time in my life was not sexual at all. I was so confused as to how in the world could he be so sweet and not be sexual at all. Honestly, I thought, He must be gay. I learned he definitely was not after we got married.

He was a virgin, he didn't know at all what to do. He was adorably clueless! We would go to his uncle's house, walk down the dirt road hand in hand. It was Sweet! I had never experienced this feeling in my whole life. I prayed it would never end. He took me down the little dirt road to where his granny's house was. It was so beautiful, caving in and not safe to enter, but he told me everything he could. He told me about where the piano sat, the cellar, and how he just loved his granny.

We also went bowling 2 nights. I had so much fun! Before my wreck I loved bowling, but after my wreck I didn't go again till Brian took me. I got the lightest ball and squatted and rolled it between my legs. I'm sure I looked plum stupid! After my wreck I had very bad coordination and balance problems. Then he got the great idea to stand behind me and help support me, and my arm and throw it correctly. I did much better with his help. I have no idea what my score was and I didn't care. It was so nice to have a man gently embrace me like he did! I melted like butter in his arms.

After four days of dating he asked me to marry him. I said, Yes! After all I had been through it could only get better.

He lived in Abilene, Texas. He called me all the time. After my wreck I was disabled. I knew I would never be the same and I wanted a life. I knew something was wrong with him after I got to know him November 1999—December 2000. I didn't care. I loved him. So, December 22nd of 2000 we got married. Neither of us had money so we eloped in Eureka.

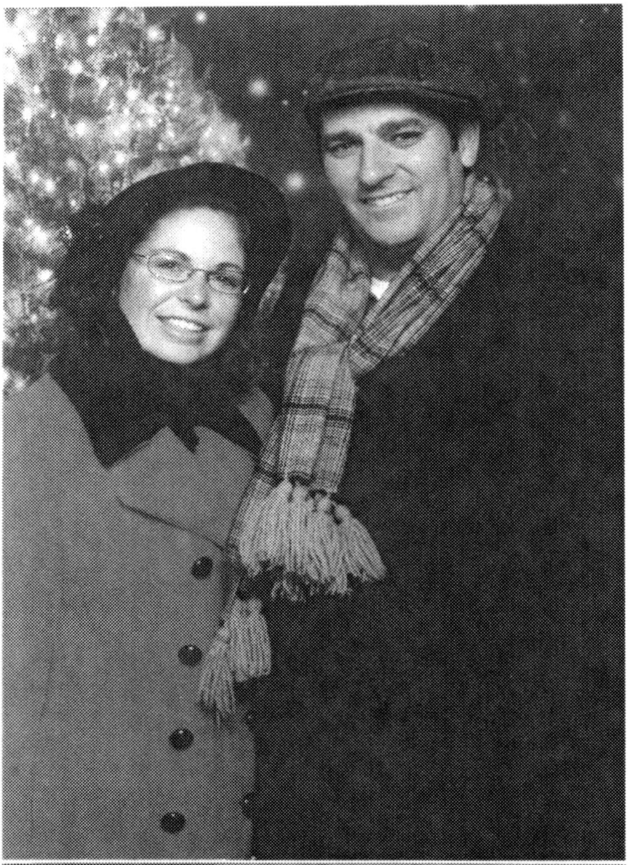

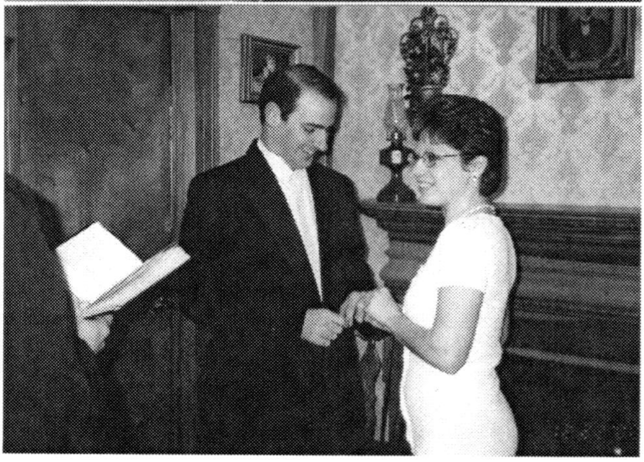

The first year of our marriage I did everything at home; cooked, cleaned and took care of everything around our home. I mowed our yard because Brian had allergies and it would cost so much for the doctor and medicine it wouldn't have been worth it. I love to work in the yard so I would have fought over him letting me do it anyway. Brian was working at a retail chain as a door greeter 10pm—7 am. It was awful! He slept all the time.

We just got married December 22nd. He wanted a wife for Christmas. He got me. It was Christmas Day all of a sudden he went from Happy as can be to severely depressed. I thought Oh No! I asked him, What's wrong?. He said, He really got depressed when Christmas was over and everyone took the tree and decorations down. I said, Let's leave them up! So, we have always had a Christmas tree in our living room ever since! My theme in our house is Christmas. What better way is there to celebrate the birth of Christ than every day of the year? You know how happy and jolly a home is when it's decorated for Christmas, mine is that way all the time.

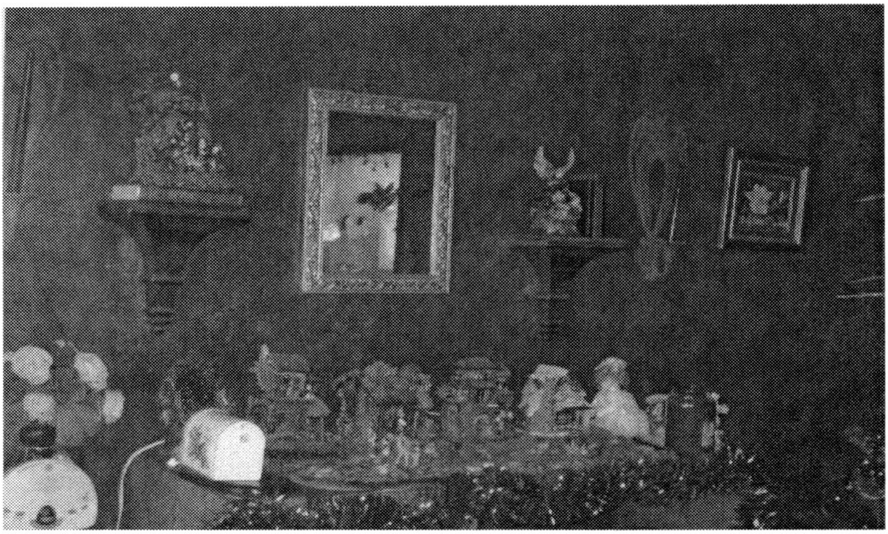

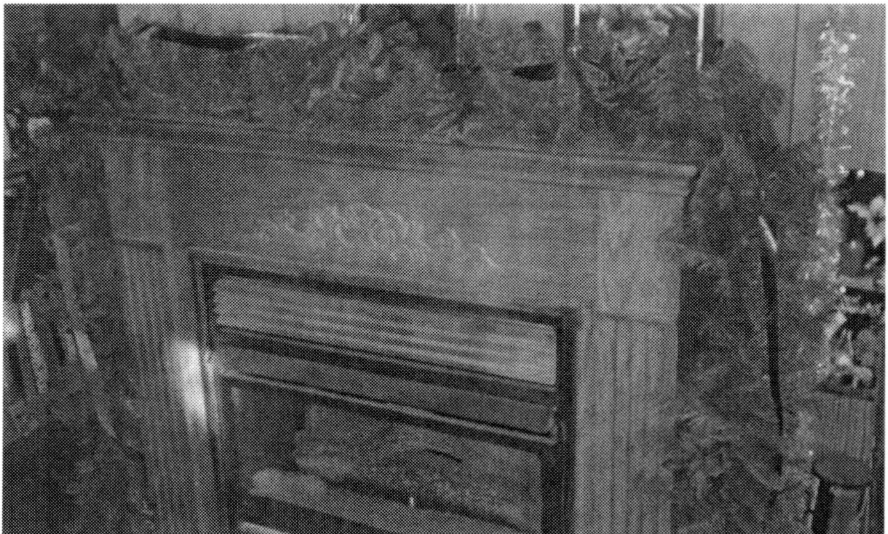

Speaking of our home Brian bought our home the day before we got married. I owed a ¼ of a million dollars in medical bills so there was no way we could get approved for a loan because I had to file medical bankruptcy. Brian moved into our house November 25th, 2000. He was renting an apartment just outside of Berryville. When we got married and I moved in we already had everything! Brian decided when he was 25 years old he was going to get married, so he filled his closet with everything you could possibly imagine needing for when he got married to give to his wife. Well, that lucky woman was ME!! He bought all sorts of Christmas colored kitchen and bath towels, 8 oven mittens, 5 sets of silver ware, iron and ironing board, 3 Christmas broaches, a mixer, 4 snow globes, 4 sets of glasses, 2 clocks, electric can opener, welcome mat, red table cloth, wall mirror, coffee pot, Panasonic Microwave, toaster oven, 2 sets of Revere Ware pots and pans, 3 kitchen canister sets, beautiful decorative glass bowls of every size. And, that's just some of the big stuff. My whole life I never had a toaster oven or anything new. I was in awe that a man could do so much for a wife he didn't even know or if he could ever find one. He had lots and lots of trouble finding a girl. He is so unbelievably sweet they thought he had evil intentions. I got to be the lucky one. He was so desperate to find a wife when he met me, he didn't care about my past. He wanted a wife, he was afraid he would die and never get to experience love, sex, and all that good stuff God created man and woman for. Boy, did God ever know what he was doing. Where I needed all this attention, Brian gave it, no problem. Where he needed to be mothered and taken care of, for me it was no problem.

Work

Our daily life was a mess. Brian worked 10pm—7am as a door greeter at a retail chain. He did okay at this job at first. They only had him stand inside the door, then go outside for a few minutes. He started to get really bad leg cramps from having to stand in one place. He was not made by God to be an overnight worker. It was a horrible way to start out a married life! I had to hang blankets on the windows in our bedroom so it would be dark so he could sleep during the day. He would sleep till 8 pm, 13 hours! I would have to have his bath ready for him to get into. Feed him whatever supper he wanted, which had to be one of 8 very specific meals. Autistic people are very picky when it comes to eating. The texture of the food or the color, it could be anything! He would not willingly take a shower, the only showers he would ever take, was whenever we would go camping and a shower was the only thing available.

Soon, they began asking him to clean the lobby and watch the door. Brian is a do only one thing at a time person so this really frustrated and fatigued him. He began to sleep every minute he was home. I would get him up just in time to take a really fast bath, (he really prefers to soak), eat one of his meals, and, leave for work. My married life was getting even worse. I remember thinking...I'm just his maid, and we sleep in the same bed, but, at different times. There was no way I could sleep while it was daylight. God had me wired. God would wake me up everyday just before my alarm went off, and still does.

Brian's lady managers would get so frustrated with Brian because he was so overwhelmed by duties that seemed easy to them. They also had Brian pushing carts, which was a very bad idea. Brian looks like he would be very strong but looks can be deceiving. This made him even more tired, I didn't think that was possible. He already slept all the time.

They finally had him watch the back door to see who came in and out to make sure nothing was stolen while the construction crew went back and forth. Well, I know Brian, and he wouldn't know if they were stealing it or not. He thought because they were on the construction crew they might have needed it for their job. He wouldn't have known whether they bought it or not. I asked him and he said he wouldn't have even thought to ask to see a receipt. Even if he had he wouldn't have the nerve to ask. He is not assertive at all. He is just plain sweet, he doesn't think evil of anyone. Because of his Autism he is extremely easy to take advantage of. After the back door, he went back to the 10pm—7am door greeter. He did alright at this job till they had him do multiple duties. He just couldn't find a job that worked for him. I wish I would have known what I do now, hind sight is 20/20. They moved him for the fifth time to being a toy stocker 10pm—7am.

Bless his heart. he had a lot of problems with this job. He does not have reasoning skills like you and I, so putting up toys was very difficult. He would, for example, have a box of matchbox cars and he would look for an exact match not realizing the box was an assortment. Another example is he couldn't reason out the bike tubes were small to large and could have different numbers.

He would get lots of small toys with no home and realize they must be strip clip items. He would have to zigzag up and down each isle looking for it, because when this retail store puts an item on a strip clip it could be anywhere. There was not a pattern for Brian to follow. Autistic people need patterns to follow. He took forever finding all the homes for these items. His manager was extremely frustrated so they finally moved him a sixth time to the register.

At first, this was the perfect job for Brian. His register came out perfect every single time, except it was still 10pm-7 am so he still slept all the time.

Then his manager suddenly required him to do other things and quick! He would have to go fill the candy wall and zip back to his register every time a customer was there, then, zip back when he was finished checking the customer out. I know Brian, he is not very observant, I'm sure this was very difficult for him. We are talking about a do one thing at a time person.

When he is allowed to do that one thing, he is very good. I would challenge you to find a better worker. Now, start adding duties and, you throw him for a loop! Next, they had him clean all 23 registers, then, he had to get the trash, then get the cardboard. At first, he did the jobs just like he was told. Then Brian came up with a great idea instead of having to go to each register 3 times why not do all the jobs at each register? They said, No. You have to do the duties one at a time. He thought it was dumb! I have to agree with him on this one. He would have to do all this and watch for customers and go back and forth in a matter of seconds. He started feeling puny and felt like he could pass out but never did, glory to God! He did, however, fall asleep putting up cigarettes at the register one day after sleeping 13 hours at home.

He already slept every minute he wasn't working except to get a bath and eat. He zoned out constantly at work since his duties were increased. There were constantly mistakes in his register. He got several pink slips for them, they gave you a pink slip if your drawer didn't come out perfectly. He also got written up twice and had 2 verbal warnings. They told him he was real close to getting fired but they were trying to keep him as long as they could before they did. Brian is so sweet nobody would have the heart to fire him that's how he kept this job for so long. One more write up and he would be gone.

Once again, they were asking him to do way more than he could handle. I now know it's because of his Autism that's why he couldn't! People would say to me maybe he is lazy. I knew better, for he is a very hard worker if he knows what's going on. I figured it had something to do with his brain damage. We both had brain damage; his was from being born a blue baby and mine was from my near fatal wreck. Anyway he doesn't have any stand up for himself skills. I'm sure it didn't occur to him to explain that he was only capable of doing one thing at a time. I didn't know that back then or I would have told them myself.

They changed his job yet again they kept pulling him off the register to zone the grocery department. Then, they had him blocking instead of zoning, which got him confused. The job of blocking was exact opposite of zoning. Zoning meant pulling everything to the front. Blocking meant push everything to the back so the stockers could see how much room there was to stock. I never had to block when I worked for this retail chain so I had to have him try to explain it to me. I could see the frustration, he couldn't explain. So, I said, Show me. His body relaxed and he drew the process on a piece of paper. It made sense when I had him show me. Then he had to help stock. After a while he would go back to the register, but he would be thrown for a loop. This got on his nerves and made him more worn out. He finally got fed up after two years of being pushed all over trying to find a job he could handle. If they just had him do one thing he would have been fine. For a while, he does do fine until one day his body decides it's had enough. There are no warnings when this happens. He was having a regular blood pressure of 150/100 and hard abdominal pains that felt like hard ulcers, and an occasional rapid pulse. He snacked constantly and chewed gum constantly to boost his energy to handle the job. He gained a lot of weight in the process 170lbs to 190lbs. I would have never guessed that gum would give anyone energy. When you are Autistic anything can cause an abnormal reaction.

Finally on April 2, 2002 he quit his job at the retail store, and began working at a Green Forest filling station on April 5th of 2002. He started out this job okay. It took him a very long time to get everything down pat though.

He worked as a cook in the Fried chicken part, the sandwich assembler in the sub part, the pizza maker in pizza part, and occasionally served ice-cream in the ice-cream part.

He started feeling fatigued and got slower and slower. His hours were 2pm-11pm. He started out sleeping till 10am, then it got even worse after a couple of months, even though he started getting the hang of his job it wasn't long before he began sleeping the whole time he was home again. What a bummer! I was looking forward to having a little quality time with my man. We did get to play games a lot till he got tired again. It wasn't his fault though. At work he began being very confused. He couldn't sequence things right, and forgot how to do almost everything he had learned to do!

When he did the sub's he did okay with white and wheat breads. When they added Banana Nut Bread, Italian, Hawaiian breads etc. he was lost! He had to remember all the unusual ways to prepare each one. He said they had written down how to put all the stuff on the sandwiches, but not how to make all the different breads. The bread was already in rolls he just had to know what spices went on what kind of bread. I'm sure this really had him stumped. He can't make the connection between which spices were what flavor. He is not a person who knows his way around a kitchen, must less know his spices. He also had a hard time keeping up with the soups and salads. He just could not remember the sequence to preparing each one of them. Once again he was being asked to remember the sequence to doing several different things. At least he knew most of the time which part he was going to work in. They had different shirts for each station so he had to keep up with where he was to work so he wore the correct shirt. Amazingly he only wore the wrong one a couple of times. There were lots of customer complaints about the way he made sandwiches.

He was taught to give the sandwich a slight toss at the register, one customer told him You threw it at me! He said, I was taught to give it a slight toss. She was very upset! I can't believe Brian actually stood up for himself...kind of?

He also had a horrible time finding different products in the freezer.

Some of the stuff had a pattern but there were lots of things stuck here and there. This would have been hard for the average person. Add Autism and it is unreasonable to expect the person to grasp it.

He did okay in the fried chicken most of the time but the pace and pressure were way too fast for him. That's the only station he worked in where he would come home filthy and stinky! He looked like he had a day full of fights with the flour bin. I would always have to wash his fried chicken shirts over and over just to get the ground in flour and grease out.

He did his best job in the pizza. There were a few times where he messed up, as usual, but not near as many. There were not a bunch of steps to have to remember like the other stations.

He began feeling like he was falling all over himself. He couldn't concentrate and blew it all over the place, for example… he would leave his cab light on in his car and run the battery dead. He locked his keys in his car once and had to get an officer to let him in his own car. On top of all this some elderly lady hit his parked car while he was working one day.

Because of the pace and pressure he snacked and drank pop constantly in order to handle the jobs again. He gained even more weight after gaining 20lbs at the retail chain for the same reason. He now weighed 210lbs! His blood pressure averaged 150 over 100, had really hard, dull stomach pains. He was severely fatigued. He was sleeping 13 hours a day again and zoned out at work because he was so tired. He was constantly going to the bathroom, he was having really bad prostate problems, he felt like he had to urinate but couldn't. I'm sure they didn't believe him, they probably thought we are not paying him to be in the bathroom all the time. He was also just as bad at home we even had to move from our full sized bed to our king size bed so he wouldn't wake me up constantly every time he got up to try to urinate. I thought he had just formed a habit, I was determined to break him of it! If he didn't start to urinate a few minutes after trying I would grab him by the hand and escort him out of the bathroom. Needless to say, he got fired from the filling station March 17, 2003. This made the third time he had gotten fired from a job!

Disability

He applied for disability on January 23rd, 2003 before he got fired. He was told he could only work 30 hours. We had a house payment, and a car payment, and a loan payment. Brian got loan upon loan to make cassette tapes of him singing gospel music. He thought he would make it big but God wasn't in it. I knew I would have to do something. So I decided I would work cleaning house like I used to. Social Security allowed me to work and make as much money as I could for a trial work period of nine months. So I did! I cleaned four houses a day for six days a week. I sure made good money and I had to just to survive. I did not have a problem finding people to clean for. I had such a good reputation from cleaning houses before my wreck. They seemed to come at me fast when they found out I was cleaning again. My check was $740, and Brian was only making $560. Our house payment was $340.69, the car payment was $150, and the loan was $120 for a total of $610.69. That left $689 for all our bills, car gas, groceries, and everything else. It was tight. But thanks to God I was able to clean.

I didn't think he would get disability. I sure prayed he would! I was beginning to see how he probably would not be able to hold a job for long. It was just a matter of time before nobody would hire him because of not ever being able to handle a job.

He received disability on July 16th, 2003! He didn't have to be jobless for a full year like you were supposed to. Thank God! I wouldn't have been allowed to work for that long.

We began to go camping a lot. It was so fun I finally had some awake time with my husband.

Doctors

This subject is very important to my husband so I pray that what I write meets his expectations. If it doesn't he will drive me batty till it does. I'm going to just copy what he wrote about this subject only changing the pronouns. I will also add my comments.

First I'll tell you about his experience with his Urologist. He started doing somewhat worse that January and the medicines he took began to work less. By June, the Septra that always did the trick when all other medicines failed, for the first time ever quit working completely.

He had been to several Urologists between the summer of 2003 and the summer of 2004 that did him no good at all. He went to a Urologist in Missouri who saw him one time. He refused to treat him till he got records from a previous Urologist. He said There aint no way a 35 year old can have a prostate problem! No way! Brian wanted to be treated that day because he knew what the records would say were completely off! He finally found one that believed him about the prostate in October 2004 that would actually do something about it.

In July of 2003, a urologist Brian went to agreed he had a prostate problem, till an ex-urologist who (tried to treat him for an overactive bladder) convinced this urologist that he was right. This is exactly what he was afraid would happen. His ex-urologist was wrong of course and ended up causing the problem to get even worse. That's why he was trying to find another one. The urologist he was currently seeing insisted he have a Urodynamics study done before he did prostate surgery. The doctors office insisted he do it awake. Brian has an extreme over-sensitivity to pain so this was an outrageous request. He knew he wouldn't be able to handle it and tried to tell them. He went ahead and cooperated, but the pain was so excruciating he screamed loudly through the whole procedure which they never got to finish. At first, the assistant was not very comforting to him until she saw the experience was overbearing to him. She then put her hand on his shoulder and said, Come on! Come on! Just a little bit longer! We're almost there! Just half way to go! Then the nurse inserting the catheter said, I'm sorry! I'm going to have to quit! I'm hurting him too much! Brian said the assistant had tears in her eyes. I'm sure she was trying not to cry.

    We explained what happened to this doctor but he insisted that Brian retake the test and do it awake. Talk about torture, I thought health care professionals were supposed to have the patient's best interest in mind. Apparently not this one, he didn't seem to care!

    This Urologist also told him Brian he had Interstitial Cystitis. This doctor tried to get him to take Elavil and eventually Amatryptoline, which caused Brian sharp shooting pains in the urethra. Everything he tried to give Brian made him even worse. Brian told him about the part of the test she did get done, how it indicated He still had 333ml left in the bladder after voiding 188ml. Brian said, I have a retention problem, not an incontinence problem.

    We finally dropped this guy and went to another doctor in Missouri.

    This doctor tried to make Brian do a Cystogram awake! Brian flipped out! The pain was so excruciating Brian accidentally kicked the foot rest off the exam table. Brian wasn't able to do the Cystogram this time either. It was so frustrating for us to warn all these Doctors, but none of them would listen. I even got mad at Brian this time. I remember thinking, you're not even trying! I thought it can't be that bad. I didn't know Brian was Autistic yet or that an over sensitivity to pain was one of the symptoms. Looking back I feel so bad for not believing my husband. He hasn't lied before, why would he have started right then? I now know he is Autistic and has an over-sensitivity to pain.

Finally after all this, in October 2004 we finally found one who believed him. God is so awesome! All things work out for the good of those who love the Lord. It was a two-hour drive to his office but it was worth the drive. It was a beautiful drive and gas did not cost near as much as it does now. He was an older man so I thought he would know by experience what his urinary problem was. Everyone in his office treated Brian as if he were a child. He would give everyone of the nurses he liked a hug, sometimes more than once. They were fine with it. They thought it was sweet.

Hospital

In November 2004 the Urologist Brian went to decided to do a Urethrogram only this time the Urologist said he would use Anesthesia at the hospital which was right across the street. We tried to tell him how badly he handled IV's. I warned him as best I could, but he didn't completely understand. We did talk the hospital into doing the gas, but they insisted they were going to do the IV first. Because of his Autism he thinks they are just being mean to him, he can't see the medical reason behind them insisting on the needle first. With all his medical knowledge from taking so many years of medical related classes in college you would think he would understand. But he didn't. It was confusing to me to see him not understanding a simple procedure like this one.

We bugged the lab about this and they had him talk to a nurse on the phone after they finished doing his blood test he was required to have. Boy howdy they had a hard time getting him through this. When Brian has to have a blood test he told me, it feels as if he's been stuck with a steak knife. This time when he went in the lab an old lady helped him out. It comforted him to have a granny type nurse with lots of compassion to help him get through it. The second time he had to get a blood test when he went in for surgery a nice young girl did the blood test and she was good. They still asked her if she needed more help, but she said, No. I think I've got it. It's okay. Brian wanted to give her a hug afterwards but he was afraid she wouldn't understand so he skipped it, but it really depressed him not to.

We should have trusted the Lord and asked Him to do what Brian needed, but we went to the pro-op waiting room, and asked for them to let Brian talk to the Anesthesiologist. They gave him a nurse to talk to on the phone. It is very hard for Brian to trust the Lord for something like this. Being a concrete thinker Faith has him stumped. He assures me that he has put his faith in the Lord to save him. I can't seem to understand how this can be. I'm sure all Autistic people do not go to hell. God has to have a provision for people like Brian who in some areas in life he is like a two year old.

She tried to console him, but he was so persistent with insisting that he have the gas first. They finally said okay! I'm not going to say that its not going to hurt, but I will assure you that the IV person will try as hard as they can not to hurt you. They will be as gentle as possible. He finally realized he had lost this battle. It is very important to be honest as possible when you are dealing with an Autistic person. If they would have said, It won't hurt a bit! they would have lost every bit of trust he had in them. It would have been even worse than it was. It is nearly impossible to treat a person who doesn't trust you.

Three days later he went to the pre-op for anesthesia to put him to sleep for the Urethrogram x-ray and VCUG x-ray.

He met this IV-helper nurse that was really nice. Autistic people really do need to be treated as if they were a child. Being in a hospital is even more scary to them than it is for your the person even the average child. He told this IV helper how scared he was, and she got all pumped up and said reassuringly Don't you worry! We're going to get through this! You're going to be, okay! Brian said, Do you think you can handle someone like me? The IV-helper said, Yeah! That's no problem! We can handle this! We can get you through this! You'll see! You're going to be all right! When it was time to go the IV-helper said, Come on and come with me and I'll show you where to go! It's okay!

You're going to be all-right! You'll see! It's going to be okay! It is also very important that the nurse stay positive and upbeat. If the Autistic person senses the slightest doubt, you're in for an experience you wish your were not part of. Brian will completely freak out, how he acted before is nothing in comparison.

The IV-helper showed him to his room and said, Now come in here and change into this gown and let me know when you're ready! He changed into his gown and when he was ready he called her back into the room.

The IV-helper came back into the room. The IV-sticker came in after her. They got on each side of the bed next to the sides of his arms. They stood next to the railing real close like they were trying to trap him in case he gave them any problems. The IV-helper was there to hold his hand when the nurse stuck him with the IV. He looked back and forth at both of them, in panic!

He particularly looked at the helper in fear hoping for sympathy. He started frantically asking questions and looked over at the helper he liked (as a child would look to its mother) and said Is the anesthesiologist going to come in!!!? I wasn't in there but I'm sure he was hysterical.

He was looking for comfort, she paused for a second then she went outside of the room and stood in front of a table leaning against it. I have a feeling she was just starting and didn't know how to deal with a patient like Brian. She looked straight at him from there, and at the same time another helper came in. The nurse said, Mind if we have a substitute? Brian said, I guess not. In reality he really did mind! He wanted the original helper, but he went along with it anyway, he just didn't know what to say? He just wasn't blessed with the ability to stand up for himself. I'm sure he was terrified. His security blanket nurse he was comforted by left the room.

The nurse began to feel his arm and he looked at her frantically! She said, Just looking for a spot. I'm not putting it in yet. Then he looked at the other helper he wasn't as comfortable with and the nurse said, Switch sides! They switched sides. Then they switched back. Then the nurse felt his arm again and said, Now look over there at her and hold her hand, and, I'm going to stick it in Right Now!!!! He looked at the second helper frantically and screamed the instant the nurse stuck the IV in his arm. Brian, like most Autistic people is easily confused; this was an excellent tactic to use on him. It didn't do much for his anxiety disorder though I'm sure.

He was crying and hyperventilating even after he was stuck. He was desperate for the anesthesiologist to get there. I'm sure it felt like an eternity to him. Autistic people are very impatient, they want whatever it is now!

Then the nurse said, Here, why don't we give you some Oxygen? I think it might help. I think you really need it right now. Now breathe this and try to relax! Try is right! Try to relax. There was no way Brian could relax. She had no idea what kind of trauma he just endured. When Brian is stuck with an IV it feels like he's been stuck with a butcher knife.

He was given the oxygen, and it helped a little, but he was still frantic! The anesthesiologist finally came in to give him the gas several minutes later. The original helper observed the whole thing from the table outside of the room.

When the Anesthesiologist put him to sleep they did an Urethrogram and a VCUG. He woke up in the x-ray room and two girls asked him to try to urinate through the tube into the catheter bag. They said, It's really going to hurt but we need you to try anyway. He tried to urinate several times but he was unable to go. Then they said they would remove the catheter and have him try to go in a plastic urinal. They said, Okay! We're going to take it out now! You ready! He said, Okay. They took him by surprise and removed it quickly. You don't ever want to do anything as painful as this in slow motion to anyone much less an Autistic person. It just prolongs the misery!

Then he tried to go in the plastic urinal with no luck. Then they said, Now hold on to me and we're going to take you off the bed to take you to the bathroom. He tried going several times standing up with still no luck They said, Do you think it would help if you sat down? He said he Didn't know, but he would try. Brian is a very easy-going person. He would do anything he could to make sure he didn't disappoint you, as long as it wasn't un-biblical. He still had no luck, then they gave up.

They had him get back on the table and a guy came and took him into the recovery room. I'm sure this terrified Brian! He needed nurturing and they sent a man to take him to the recovery room. Men frighten Brian but I'm sure they did this because he is a pretty heavy guy for a woman to push. They may not even have the ladies push anybody.

He told the recovery room nurse what happened and she said that was unusual because most people were able to go after the dye was pumped into them. The nurse said, You are the first one in seven years to ever have this problem. He had to wait 45 minutes in the recovery room for the doctor to come after already waiting 20 minutes in the x-ray room trying to use the restroom but not being able to go. He really needed to go bad in there but he couldn't. The recovery room nurse brought him a plastic urinal to urinate in just in case. He wasn't able to go. He finally saw the doctor who told him he retained abnormally large amounts of urine and said he had an overactive sphincter and that was part of the reason he couldn't go. I'm sure this news relieved Brian to a certain extent. Brian, like anybody likes to have a name for his problem. Brian is a hypochondriac in my opinion. Anybody could be talking about whatever and if the thing they are talking about fits his symptoms at all he thinks he has the very same problem.

I was in the recovery room with him. I held his hand and scratched his scalp while they took the IV out. It was huge and really long. No wonder it hurt him so bad. I've never seen one that big before.

Finally, he said, Is there a bathroom in here? A nurse told him where it was. He went in there and had trouble at first, but then he went like a race horse and it was as if the whole thing never happened. It really helped to know what was wrong, then he was able to urinate.

After this, he got dressed and another nurse wheel-chaired him to our car.

The doctor scheduled him to come back in a month. He had so many problems urinating he saw him in three weeks. I told him, We're tired of medicine and we want to have a surgery to fix the problem. Brian tried to talk him into a TURP, but he decided to do a TURVN

(Trans-urethral Resection of the vesicular neck([bladder-neck) to create an opening into the bladder.

The doctor scheduled this operation for December 13th of 2004.

When he arrived at the hospital, he told the anesthesiologist to tell his doctor if he finds something and he sees prostate blockage, remove it. He said he would tell the doctor.

When he first got to the Pre-op waiting room he saw his favorite IV helper. He was so excited. His original IV nurse gave him a hug, then told him she had to go to a meeting so, she said he'd have to have a substitute. This kind of upset him even though she said I could go in there with him this time because they were short on help. He felt he had to go to the bathroom several times before his scheduled pre-op appointment even though he was not allowed any liquids after midnight. He is unable to empty his bladder completely. He apologized to the IV helper and told her he couldn't help it. He asked her for a hug and she gave him one. Brian is a very odd Autistic person; apparently he is one of the few Autistics who like to be touched. He hasn't always been this way. When he was an infant he would stiffen up when anybody other than his mother tried to hold him. If Brian likes you and you don't give him a hug, he thinks there's something wrong.

The IV helper was ready and said, Do you remember how to get back there? He said, Kind of, but, you might want to show me anyway. So she took him back there and said goodbye. He wanted her to stay and be the IV helper again because she did such a good job the first time, even though she just watched from outside. He almost begged her to stay but he didn't say anything. She was working at the waiting room desk that day, and he figured she had to be there. Because of his Autism that's probably one of the few times he has ever taken into account what was going on with someone else.

I helped him this time, but according to him, he didn't do nearly as well. He screamed loudly, and all the nurses turned and looked at him grimly. Since the anesthesiologist set in part of the time with him, Brian asked, there isn't any chance you'd give me the gas first, is there? but the anesthesiologist just kept saying, No. They waited for a few minutes after he had been stuck, then they gave him the gas. After his surgery, he had to wait several minutes before he could get a room upstairs. While he was there, they told him the doctor did find prostate blockage in the bladder neck, so he did a TURP, a TURVN, a Sphincterotomy. This made Brian very happy. He likes to be able to put a name to his problems. I think he likes to talk about what he has been through. I think it is truly amazing what the Lord has brought Brian through. Even more amazing he would lead him to me! I am so blessed to be his wife. I never have to be bored with the same old same old. My life is an adventure!

When he went into the in-patient care on 3rd floor west, the two nurses he had on the very first day were very nice to him. The next day, the Charge nurse, the RN, and the Nurse Aide were very ugly to him. It is very important that you are not ugly with an Autistic person.

The night before, one of the nice nurses talked to him about all the different ways the nurses would accommodate him the next morning in helping him with tasks he would normally be able to fulfill himself, but would not be able to do for himself while he was in the hospital because of his weakness and condition after the surgery. The subject came up about baths eventually and this girl said, There are no tubs. There are no showers. You will have to ask for a sponge bath and your day nurse will take care of this for you. If you do not ask you will not get one because they will only do it if you ask.

At 3am in the morning a nice young lab girl came into Brian's room to give him a blood test. She said she'd try to find a place in his right arm to do it even though the IV was in the right arm because Brian is particularly oversensitive to pain in his left arm. She finally decided that she was going to have to do it in his left arm and apologized for having to do so. However, she stuck the needle in a place that no one's ever done it before. Instead of going to the direct middle of his left arm she went off to the corner just above the mid arm and to the left. She was very gentle with her stick and Brian was amazed. He barely felt it, and normally in that arm he is in excruciating pain. This girl was very good and very friendly, too. Brian really liked her. She was very nice to him.

The next day, the Charge nurse came in and Brian asked her questions like the ones he asked the nurse the night before.

He finally remembered to ask her to give him a sponge bath, and she said, Okay. I can do that. It will probably be a while. It may be 2 or 3 hours before I can make it in here. He waited 3 hours for her to come and did not see her. So he called the nurse's station and asked if she could come in and give him a sponge bath. They said, It will be a little while. She has some other things she has to take care of first. Then she could come in there He said, Okay. He was just doing as he was told from the nurse the night before.

About a minute later, after talking to the nurse's station, suddenly the RN comes in the room in a rage. She said, You know! You could do this yourself if you wanted to! All you have to do is get out of bed and jump in that chair over there and you could do all this yourself! You don't have to have us give you a bath! You can do it yourself! (Notice: There was a big sign on the wall in big black bold print that said, DO NOT GET OUT OF BED! A NURSE WILL COME AND ASSIST YOU!) She had no idea of his over-sensitivity to pain.

The RN angrily tried to get him out of bed, but couldn't do it herself because his catheter had him in such excruciating pain that he could barely move.

The nurse's aide walked to the door and the RN said, Come help me with him! I'm having a hard time getting him out of bed! That should have been a clue to her that he was not able to do it himself.

They both helped him, but because of the pain, he could barely move. The nurse's aide said, Now try to set up in bed. We've got to try to make it now. While going through several steps, he was screaming in pain in the process and the RN said to the nurse's aide, Why is it hurting him so much?! The other nurse said, I don't know. I Being his wife, I thought I know what's wrong, It wouldn't have been half the traumatic experience if they were a little bit nice to him. The nurse's aide told Brian, Now try to swing your legs over. We need to try to make it now. Now try to get down. Take your time. Be careful now. Good. We finally got you stood up. Now we need to get you to the chair. Being nice to Brian is what you have to do if you want any help from him. Be mean and he is terrified, he couldn't help if he wanted to.

At this point, the RN says abrasively, You better hope you're able to do all this stuff yourself, because if you're not you'll never get out of here, because I'm not going to let you go until you prove to me you can! You're going to be here a long time if you don't, so, you better hope you can! This is the wrong way to deal with an Autistic person. Brian needed to be comforted not yelled at!

The nurse's aide then took him to the chair. It took several steps just to get him in the chair. Then she said, See, you could have done it yourself if you wanted to. All you had to do is get in this chair and bathe yourself. You don't need us.

The nurse's aide then said, Now remove your gown. You can get your top and I can get your legs.

About the time the nurse's aide was done, when Brian thought they were going to help him back in bed, the RN suddenly says abrasively, I'm going to come back here and I'm going to drag you out of that bed later, and, we're going to walk you down that hall! I'm not going to tell you when! He begged her, Please, Can we just go and get this over with now? I don't want to have to go through that again after I already went through it once. Please, Can we just do it now? He was filled with panic!

The RN left him setting down in the chair. She said, Hold on. I have to go down the hall real quick. Let me go ask and I'll find out. I'll be back in a minute. The nurse's aide left a couple of minutes after she did. Brian waited for 20 minutes and did not see her. Because of his frustrations, we tried to call the charge nurse to talk to her because we had a complaint about the RN. The nurse should have at least told him the truth. I thought they needed to know just how uncompassionate their employees were to my husband.

The Charge nurse finally came in and talked to us. He told her that the RN said he could have given himself a bath if he had wanted to. All the Charge nurse said was, Yeah. I know, but you probably could have. It just would have been very painful. I nearly came out of my skin. She had no idea how traumatic the whole ordeal was for him. I watched it,

I knew. It was real; I no longer thought Brian was just being a baby! If I were her and saw the horrific pain her nurses were putting him in with no compassion, they would have been fired immediately. Nurses are so hard to find they probably have to keep them or go nurseless!

Brian suspected that the Charge nurse may have set these two nurses up to this because of the way they came in like clockwork after he asked for the Charge nurse at the nurse's station. Brian has been through so many horrible situations it's really easy for him to make these assumptions. The statement the Charge nurse made after this when he talked to her made him think even more that she was behind it. She was very unremorseful, and he figured she must have been using these two for revenge for asking her for a sponge bath.

Later that day all three of them came to adjust his catheter, which lasted several minutes. According to Brian it felt like they were jerking it in every move they made with it. He was screaming in pain because of it. He finally reached out for the Charge nurse's hand in desperation for mercy and sympathy. She jerked her hand away and her arm, then stepped back. Then she started working with his catheter all over again. Then he reached for the RN's hand, and she did the same thing. Then he reached for the nurse's aide's hand, and she did it too! All three of them kept messing with his catheter for several more minutes without having any sympathy whatsoever for his feelings and his oversensitivity to pain. Brian desperately needed a little compassion here. Everyone around him shunned him instead of comforting him.

That night, the nurse he was comfortable with finally came in and he was relieved. At first he slept well, but woke up in the middle of the night and could not sleep. He was crying at 3 am in the morning, and she said, Are you alright? and, he said, No. He told her what happened with the three nurses and said, If I just hadn't asked for a sponge bath, this whole thing would never have happened. Then, she said, Now, don't you think you've done anything wrong. You've done nothing but be kind and polite ever since you've been here. I've got nothing but good reports about you. This nurse treated Brian exactly like an Autistic needs to be treated.

She had to go over to the side of his bed and sit in a chair and rubbed his head for two hours. I know nurses don't have time to do this with every patient, but I sure am glad she did. Isn't it neat how God knew what he needed and made this nurse be able to do this for him. He was crying so hard she had to go through all this trouble to calm him down because he was petrified from the traumatic experience with the nurses, especially over them jerking their hands back when he reached out for comfort. Brian is very sensitive.

The next day, he decided to take his own bath. The nurse he was comfortable with removed his catheter 15 minutes before the day nurses came in Thank God! He could move then only he still had the IV in his arm. I told him there was a shower in his bathroom. He called the nurse's station and told them he didn't know how to move his IV without hurting himself to take a shower. The nurse at the nurse's station said, Not without a nurse's assistant your not! Besides, you have to unclip the thing in the middle of your IV first and your nurse would have to show you how to do it! The nurse's aide checked with the nurse's station to see if it was okay to take a shower. They thought the doctor was going to be there that morning. At 3 pm they found out it would be 5:30 pm before he got there. Brian is very particular about having a bath almost every day, so this really bothered him he has to have a bath almost every morning Brian decided to walk down to the nurse's station in his hospital gown with his IV still connected to his right arm to see if they would let him shower yet.

The minute he got to the edge of the nurse's station a nurse at the edge of the desk spotted him. She immediately turned around and started laughing. Brian thought she was laughing at him. Then suddenly, all the nurses turned around and started laughing. They stared at him constantly acting like they were trying to make him self-conscious and feel ashamed because he didn't have any clothes on except for his hospital gown. He was completely naked under his gown. Because of his self-consciousness this made him very uncomfortable. He thought they were trying to make him overly aware of it, so he would feel humiliated for being in a hospital gown. He felt like the laughing stock of the nurse's station. He felt like they were thinking, Look at the little cry baby in nothing but a hospital gown come to talk to us! They may have just told a joke, but they should have taken into account how they would feel if they were in his place.

The nurses' aide walked him back to his room and he asked her, Were they making fun of me? She said, No. It wasn't about you. It was about somebody else, but I'd rather not repeat what they said. This statement makes me think it was not appropriate to repeat, maybe a dirty joke.

When they got back to the room, she took out his IV. Then they went into the bathroom and she made him remove his gown in front of her. I'm sure this made him very self-conscious. Then she helped him into the shower regardless of the fact he was able to walk. The fact that she did this in general did not bother Brian. It's the fact that they were going to make him let them help him do it in the first place. He wondered what were they complaining about when he asked them to do it, if they were going to do it anyway. If they just didn't want to see him get completely naked in front of them, why did they complain about this, if they were going to make him take everything off in front of them whether he liked it or not? He would have been completely exposed one way or the other. Brian doesn't know if they ever complained about this he is just assuming because of how badly he was being treated. He felt like most of the nurses he ran into acted like they thought he was their property any way. They could have done anything they wanted to unless the doctor said otherwise. He already ran into one situation where one of the nurses popped in and said if they took the catheter out too early they would have to reinsert it. He really got worried! Brian begged them to knock him out and put him under the gas if they did. They said, Only if the doctor orders it we will. If not, we're just going to reinsert it if we see you are still unable to go. They acted like this made them feel somehow powerful over him, whoever they were. It just made Brian scared. I would have insisted to talk to the doctor to be sure they knocked him out.

After the doctor discharged him, he went to the nurse's station to get his papers filled out and signed. They took a long time with the papers, and, a male nurse says in a rude tone of voice, What do you want? Is there something we can help you with? He had a really ugly look on his face. Men make Brian very uneasy. As a child, they were nothing but mean to him. Then, a female nurse said in a rude tone of voice, Can I help you? He told them he was waiting for the charge nurse to fill out his paperwork. Because of his Autism, Brian tends to hover around when he is waiting for something. This makes people uneasy. When we finally got to go, a lady tried to insist on rolling him out with a wheelchair, but he wanted to walk, so he could go tell his favorite operating room nurse goodbye hoping she was at her desk. He had to leave a note because she was busy in the operating room, and the nurses at the desk said they'd make sure she got the note. They all acted very happy to see him. They all said goodbye to him and wished him good luck. They told him they hoped he felt better. That was the end of his stay for surgery and he went on home.

Brian was told after he got out of the hospital that if he still had trouble going to the bathroom, he'd probably be back in a week.

He had a follow up appointment December 20th. Between the 15th and the 20th he sent his favorite IV helper a letter about his experience on 3rd floor west. She wrote him back and said there wasn't much she could do so she gave his letter to the charge nurse to let them know what happened. I'm sure they are not supposed to write patients back. He also sent her and everyone else a Christmas card. Brian loves Christmas. We celebrate it 365 days a year. He also sent the IV sticker and his favorite nurse on 3rd floor west of the hospital a calendar that he hand made out of pictures we had taken. They are absolutely beautiful! Brian is so sweet, and very proud of his calendars. He wants to make everyone one but the ink is so expensive he limits himself to a few special people.

He went to say Hi on December 20th and gave his favorite IV helper a hug. She said he could fill out hero reports at the operating room waiting room. He told her he was for sure going to fill out one for her and give her a real good name. We went there immediately so we wouldn't forget. We both have poor short term memories.

Brian was still having problems going to the bathroom and wondered why his doctor didn't re-hospitalize him after almost having to go to the ER during Christmas break.

Bad Experiences

I am going to comment on what Brian has written so this part of the book is very repetitious. Bear with me that's how Autistic people learn. Brian doesn't realize you and I don't need repetition.

At this same hospital Brian had a bad experience with the Speech Pathology Department and what happened there reminded him of a past experience he had in Abilene, Texas, and, this caused him to get hysterical. He wrote letters to the language therapists in the Speech Pathology Department. Eventually, he wrote to his favorite IV nurses in the pre-op department begging them not to say, think, or do certain things to him in fear they would begin to act like the people who treated him bad in Abilene. Autistic people write in order to communicate. In order to help you understand what made him so frantic, I'm going to explain what happened in Abilene before I tell you what happened in the Speech Pathology department. This should help you see where he made the connection between the two incidents.

There was a man in his past that acted just like this director of Speech-Language Pathology. This man had it in for him and tried to ruin his reputation with every teacher he knew. He associated this director with this man, his 5th grade history teacher. His 5th grade history teacher attempted to turn his favorite 7th grade Special Ed English teacher against him. He told her he was retarded, but this didn't work because she thought he was a bully. He associated his IV helper with the 7th grade English teacher because she acted just like her. This English teacher used to pump him up for learning Grammar and made it very interesting. He did very well in her class. The IV helper pumped him up about having her for a nurse to distract his fear of the IV stick. This helped him do better even though he did scream and cry before they gave him oxygen so they wouldn't lose him. Because his 5th grade history teacher tried to turn his 7th grade English teacher against him, he feared the Director of Speech Pathology would try to turn his favorite IV helper against him in the same manner.

The other thing that made him delirious, the director of Speech Pathology thought he was after the women. Sexual thoughts do not occur to Brian. He wanted a woman because he is not comfortable with men. He remembered a series of bad experiences he had in college with girls saying bad things to him. He imagined that the IV helper would begin to say the same things and act like them. He also imagined the Speech Language Therapists to think similar things, but, not so bad. Here's what happened in college to make him fear these things.

I'm about to tell you the shocking, true, traumatic story that happened now to show you what shook him up. Here it goes.

The worst problems were in 1991, 1994, and, 1997-1999, but the overall problem began in 1986. He discovered he had a singing talent. His private opera voice instructor had taught him to act like a New Yorker from the 1800s and perfect it. He was very tense in all of his movements and he taught Brian to be the same way. His opera instructor and his friends in the town opera in 1987 taught Brian to walk, talk, and act like one of these people. They expected him to react to them as if it were the 1800s at all times. They taught him to speak very boldly in a low, loud voice at all times like people do on Broadway movies. They had him stand like a beam pole and walk like one too. They had him put his shoulders back and lock them into a certain position that was almost militaristic because he was in H.M.S. Pinafore. This was an opera about people on a boat that were in the navy and that's the way they did. They taught him to act robust in every way possible. They made him learn and perfect the body language and mannerisms of the extreme upper class society. They had certain ways they spoke to each other and certain ways they handled situations. They taught him to do all this exactly like them to the tee. They choreographed his body movements, which he thought he'd never get down. By the time they got through with him he was stuck that way. Wouldn't you know that after they finished molding him, the rest of society that originally thought he was retarded changed their mind and decided he must be crazy. There was a thing about body language going around in the middle class society in Texas that if you didn't do it just right and do it just like them you were considered to be suspicious and suspected to be a criminal. Their's were more lax and smooth. The opera's was more tense and concentrated. After Brian discovered his talent with his voice and met this man the problem with his body language began.

Here's how it started. In High School and College the guys began calling him a womanizer just to see if the girls would believe it. He is exactly the opposite so they'd laugh when the girls fell for it. Some of these girls thought weird things about him, and many were reluctant to be his girlfriend because of it, but the wife beater thing that was going around did not start happening to Brian until 1991. One guy called him a party animal in high school just to lead a girl on, and Brian told the girl it wasn't true, that he'd never drank a beer in his life. He never went to bars. By the way he never smoked, cussed like most people. That wasn't his way. It has never nor will it ever be his way. Do two year olds have any of these bad habits?

His first three years of college were not much worse than this, and his third year of college he went to school with mostly older people and got along great with them. By the summer of 1991, he'd taken two years of Music and one year of Medical Assisting. He only lacked a history class to graduate with an Associate in Applied Arts in Music degree. He had been going to a different campus location of this college in 1990-1991, but he had to go to the new campus location to take the history class.

When he walked in the door for the first time, to his amazement at the end of the front lobby area in front of a classroom were two girls standing right outside the classroom door that he'd never met in his life, and, they said, There's something strange about his smile! Sexual harassment! If you know Brian at all you know there isn't a sexual anything in his mind. He has to be enticed on purpose to even get him to think sexual.

In future instances, them or someone else would come up with this same remark. One time one of them suddenly came up with, He's got a swelled jaw! He's going to beat up his wife!

This began to be a problem over and over again with several different girls and he thought it was never going to end. When Brian told me about this I was very upset because Brian would never do anything bad to anybody. He won't even kill a fly. I have to. He just gets really aggravated when one bothers him. He is so cute, waving his arms and grunting. He sure would not beat up his wife. I've been married to him for 6 years and he has done no such thing to me nor will he ever, because he is not that type of a person. I've been through enough abuse. I can tell if someone has it in them.

During the 1992-1993 school year he went to a technical college and took Business and Medical Transcription and had classes with mostly older people and had no problems whatsoever, but he went back to the other college to finish his degree in Medical Assisting when he saw he wasn't going to get a job as a Medical Transcriptionist.

This same thing also happened in 1994, and it got even worse then.

During that year, at the very same campus, the college girls began to make the following comments. There's something strange about his smile! Sexual harassment! He has a swelled jaw! He's going to beat up his wife! A man with a low voice is a villain! He thinks he's God's gift to women! He thinks he's intelligent!

Prince Charming going out to save the day is not true love!

Hey Psycho! Nobody ever acts that nice and doesn't have something up his sleeve! The first two comments were the most commonly used.

College students made these comments. When he went to school in 1994, he also had a job at a hospital out of town as a Medical Records File Clerk where the lab girls hated his guts. They wanted to start a conspiracy to turn the people against him, but his boss knew better. One day, he was on lunch break, and they made the following comments in the lunchroom when they saw him: Look at the way he walked in the door! Weird! Look at the way he picked up the coffee pot! Weird Have you ever thought somebody might be trying to stare a hole right through you?

Being Autistic Brian has a tendency to either stare off into space in his own world or stare at someone if they catch his attention. He means nothing by it. When he stares off in his own world he can't control that, he just does it.

At about the same time, some psychic woman wrote an article in the newspaper warning that men with bushy eyebrows were villains and practically every young woman in town believed it. Brian has bushy eyebrows. Abilene, Texas is extremely caught up in New Age cult and every time a New Age cult came up with some weird idea in their head about something, he was the one that got attacked with it at school.

Most of the people that made these comments about him were people he'd never met in his life. Two girls at the one college that started in on him the very first time he walked in the door, he had no idea who they were or what was going on. They went out to ruin his reputation with other girls and did a good job of it. They turned several other girls against him telling them he was weird and telling them not to date him. Because of his Autism he has no social skills whatsoever so I'm sure everyone ostracized him.

When he found a girl here or there he was interested in either having for a girlfriend or even just being good friends with, he'd get comments like the ones I told you about like the ones earlier, such as:

I'm not your mother! I'm not your girlfriend! I'm not your hero! What do you want from me anyway? This was a comment made to him when he was just trying to get a girl to be his friend. Me however, I never wanted kids ever! God knew I'd marry one someday. Isn't that neat!!!

I don't think I need anybody that needs me! In this second example he was looking for a girlfriend. In the first comment above, however, he was just looking for a friend. These were two different girls. That is what makes relationships work, making the other person feel needed!

A third example is when he just tried to be friends with a certain girl who actually encouraged his reaction by pumping him up when they saw him and he would act pumped up back when he saw her. About the 3rd or 4th time he saw her he acted pumped about seeing her again, and then she said, Why do you like me so much?, he said, I don't know. He didn't understand why she encouraged it in the first place if she was going to be this way about it. This just confused him. He cannot make out mixed signals. He is a concrete thinker because of his Autism.

There were, however 2 other women that were about 5 or 6 years older than him that did the same thing with pumping him up to get him excited to see them. He acted pumped up back. They let him be this way toward them every-time they saw him. They never complained about it. They liked it and appreciated his reaction to them. They actually did want to be friends. These are the two women that stuck up for Brian when they saw the younger girls picking on him. Brian was always more comfortable with older people, yet he married a younger one! God has a sense of humor.

When one of his classes watched a movie on wife beaters, every girl in the classroom turned around and gave him dirty looks and looked at him like they were trying to say, And I think you're one of them!

These girls would not leave the wife beater thing alone. They insisted that was the way it was. I have news for these girls. They have no idea what they missed out on. Brian would have never hurt me, he is so gentle!

A guy told him in private to try to talk in a higher pitched voice because some of the girls thought he was a villain because he had a low voice. The guy also told him the way he tilted his shoulders back and locked them into place looked very rowdy to them and they thought it was a sign of villainous behavior as well. This is just stupid. Brian has a posture like anybody else. His was magnified by his opera training. He thought he'd never get it right enough to suit his choreographer. His peers should not have judged him. If they would have tried to get to know him, they would have found out why he looked like that.

When he majored in music a second time in 1997 he got comments from his peers such as: You're not old enough to sound like that! When you turn 33, let me know and I'll believe you sound like that! You sound like your going to punch somebody's lights out! You're not supposed to sound like that! You're not in New York on the stage! Show off! Pavarotti, the second! (Acting annoyed)

Young people acted like they thought Brian was evil because of his voice. Some of them suggested they thought the devil gave him the voice. Some people acted like they thought he was a devil because he had the voice. God is the only One capable of giving a sound so beautiful and full of magnitude to a human voice.

When he went to sing places, if there were any young girls around, they would snicker at him and act like they thought he had a psychological problem because he chose an old-fashioned 1970s or 1950s song to sing. Many young people made comments like, Do you know what year this is? Some sat back and looked at him like they thought he was evil because of what he sounded like when he sang. I think he has a beautiful voice!

People in the 30s and 40s thought his music was wonderful, it was the people ages 18-30 that thought it was so bad.

People in music used to do everything they could to stop him from making it in music because they were afraid he'd get discovered and get famous and they didn't want a nobody like him making it. He tried to make it big after we got married. He has the talent, but God wasn't the driving force, he was.

Another comment about the 1994 school year, sometimes the young girls would come up with a weird click about something, and then say, They say. They say. They also said something about rules once and he questioned them about it, but they wanted to keep it a secret as to what rules they were talking about. When they said something to him about rules he said, What rules?! They refused to tell him because they were afraid he'd figure it out.

About the wife beater business, he ran into a couple of girls sometime along in 1994 that claimed they were actually in that type of situation before and they told him he was not the type, because they'd been around people like that and they knew what he was like, and he wasn't like them at all. I'm living proof of this! He treats me with such loving care.

At the hospital outside of town he worked at, the two lab girls were caught by the maintenance worker planning a conspiracy against him to set him up to make him look like he was something he was not, and the maintenance guy went and told his boss about it right in front of him. When Brian had a Glucose Tolerance Test they harassed him for being afraid of the needle. They made it as hard as they could for him to deal with it because they wanted to be mean him.

When he had a job at the Alzheimer's Center as a Nurse Aide, he was treated like a slave by the other girls. When they found out that people thought bad things about him that I'm telling you about, they said, No! He is not that way! I will not stand for it! Brian seldom will ever tell you no. These girls picked up on this and used it to their advantage.

There were a couple of instances in 1994 when a couple of older women stuck up for Brian at college because they disapproved of the way he was being treated by the other young girls.

Before he got a job at a hospital out of town, he went through a job search organization that helped people with disabilities get jobs, but the lady that helped him said he was getting accused of sexual harassment because he was acting eccentric for a 50-year-old and accused him of being obsessed with academia. She accused the music people of being the ones he got it from. She was exactly right, it was them, but it wasn't the young ones like she thought, it was the ones in their 30s and up that he got it from. Brian wanted to fit in so bad he copied everything, but he wasn't capable of acting differently when he wasn't around these opera people. He didn't realize he needed to be different around the normal world.

Going back to the 1994 school year, there was a list of characteristics that you had to have in order to have the approval of the other girls and be worthy in their sight. Brian was told these from the girls. He would have to be...Smooth talker Jack of all trades One who can handle things.

A great problem solver, Laidback/lacksadasical One on the top of the social ladder, mainly based on the above 5 things.

In many cases, these girls would date guys you don't want to meet in your back alley, because they knew how to keep the above criteria very well.

Sometimes these guys thought they were tough because of their great strength, others were just proud of their big mouth for smooth words. Both thought that anybody that did not meet their own criteria, were freaks and a nuisance to society. Brian had a very hard time fitting in at the colleges he attended. Because of his Autism he has very odd mannerisms especially if you have no knowledge of Autism.

Most of the smooth talkers gave him problems and made comments like this, I know all the right words. I know all the right moves. Why don't you talk like me? He didn't act like them because he had no desire to!

Because of his experience with opera people, this was what his characteristic list looked like: Analytical Very good at one thing, maybe even 2 or 3, poor at everything else, Not good at knowing how to handle things Not a very good problem solver, Concrete thinker, not abstract Tense, overly concentrated/worry about a lot of things Not very high on the social ladder, lack skills in all the above areas.

All of these characteristics also just happen to be characteristics of Autism too!

Because his social characteristics did not match up to theirs exactly, they automatically regarded him as a freak, because he is not exactly like them.

At this time, there was an article in the paper about the warning signs of an abusive husband and most of the social characteristics fell upon Brian's line of tendencies, He can't remember what all was said, but it was something to the effect of this: Someone who is analytical (Brian is a concrete thinker) Someone who is loud spoken (which applied to him because of his music) Someone who likes to have things his own way (Autistics are very much this way) Certain various facial feature (That's the way God made him) Certain types of body language (Opera and Autism) Someone who is tense (Autistics are very tense, plus, he was trained to be this way by his Opera trainers) Someone with great determination in their work (Autistics are very determined with one thing at a time)

In 1995 in one of the opera productions he was in the other students, mainly the girls, acted suspicious of him because he was nervous and slow to talk in a brand new setting. When they found out he was friends with the Opera Star in charge, they changed their mind completely. Brian's involvement with the Opera has really brought him lots of heartache, but thanks to his training you should hear him sing. God has blessed him with a beautiful voice to sing praises to Him with.

Later, the same girls and a few guys invited him to a swimming party at someone's house. Brian does not go to parties nor has he ever. He must have been talked into going to fit in. They began talking about a Psychic Family Therapist they claimed was approved by a Christian college in town. The teacher they spoke of highly regarded this woman. They said the woman hypnotized some people, but with others she just used some kind of psychic therapy to get people to look into their past and disregard everything their parents told them they couldn't do in order to live as if it never happened, so they could become a new person. She also told them to do this with the bad experiences they had with other people and relive it as if nothing but good happened, so it would change the way they think and make them who they really were. They would act as if nothing had ever happened in the first place. They also said this lady was telling them they were neurotic. It was getting so weird to the point that Brian tried to find a smooth way to ease his way out of there and say goodbye without making anyone suspicious. They asked the question, Do you think this woman is taking us for our money? He almost said, Yes, I do. but he was afraid of what they might do if they were too wrapped up in it, so he tried to find a way to get out of there without offending them. He felt almost spooked on the way home when he was driving because of what had happened.

It wasn't too long after this, that a preacher got on TV and expressed his concerns about the young people in college, because he said that the

New Age people were getting into the colleges, and even into the churches. They were influencing these young people into believing a false theology and doing a very good job of it. He was worried about what was going to become of these people if it didn't stop.

One time, at a dollar store he worked at in 1998 or 1999, a guy came in with a New World Order T-shirt on and looked at Brian staring him down with dirty looks as if he were dirt beneath his turf. Brian's immediate thought was, I'm nobody's fool, New Ager! I know that you stand against everything I represent! He didn't ever say this to the guy, but he thought it in his mind very loudly and looked at the guy with a inference that this is what he was thinking.

When Brian worked at a nursing home in 1996, a girl C N A told him she had heard that there was a New Age Cult in town and they had a hideout right outside of town somewhere.

When he went to Arkansas for 2 months in 1995, he found out in a Sunday school class at a Missionary Baptist Church that all the comments that these people had been making about him all this time were the beliefs of the New Age Cult. They had certain body language and manor-isms that they nitpicked and said that if their body language was this way, they were this type of criminal, if it was that way, they were that type of criminal. They also took facial expressions and facial appearances and said, If they look this way, they're this type of criminal. If they look that way, they're that type of criminal. The teacher had a long list of matching criminal types for each facial appearance, expression, body language, manor-isms, and, the phraseology people used to tell you things, you name it. He had studied up on it and knew what they thought was what.

When he went to a University in town this 1997-1998 school year,. the choir class went on a trip to New Mexico and Colorado. When they were at church there, they were looking in the different rooms, and some of the students split up just looking around. Four boys and two or three girls went with him into a room, and the next thing he knew they started criticizing him. They asked him what kind of music he liked. He told them 1970s Pop, 1950s broad-way, and the more traditional contemporary Christian music. He told them he liked Karen

Carpenter, Barbara Streisand, and Melissa Manchester for pop singers. (He now kind of likes Mariah Carey, her older stuff before she got sexual) He also likes Anne Jillian for a pop singer.

He told them he liked Julie Andrews, Audrey Hepburn, Natalie Wood, and Julie Jones for broad-way singers. He told them he liked Dallas Holm, Dottie Rambo, and, Bill and Gloria Gaither for the gospel music.

Then they began to make fun of him, and put him down. They said he was outdated and asked him if he knew what year it was. They started naming off the heavy metal bands they listened to, and asked him why he didn't listen to their stuff because it was more modern. What's wrong with you, anyway? they'd say, Are you stuck in the 50s or something? Brian does not have the ability to stand up for himself or he would have told them he doesn't listen to that kind of music because it's satanic trash.

After a long rondevu with the music, they began asking him naughty stuff. They told him he was supposed to look for a girlfriend at the bar and not the college They asked him why didn't he go down to one of those bars where the women are naughty. They had a name for it, Why don't you go to the bar and find one of those women. They started describing what those women were like and started making sexually graphic comments about how they exploited themselves and then said, That's what you want, isn't it? Why don't you go after one of them? He told them, that was not what he wanted! He tried to get them to leave him alone, but he couldn't seem to outwit them. He didn't know how to get rid of them. He never did tell anybody they did this accept for his mother, and he wasn't sure what would happen if he did. He figured everybody would take their side. If they had any morals they Wouldn't have. I can't believe they did this in a church!

That year, he was talked into switching from Voice Performance to Music Ed. He took a Music Ed class that was just a regular Ed class elective that was required, and one day the class was watching a movie about dog beaters and wife beaters. When the part came on about the wife beaters, everyone in the class turned around and looked at him and gave him dirty looks and acted like they thought he was one of them. The way they all acted toward him was absolutely spooky to Brian. They also did this when the dog beater part came on. He's had dogs before and he never beat any of them. He has one now, and he doesn't beat it either. Is this crazy or what? Not only that, he never physically abused any girlfriend he ever had in his entire lifetime! I'm his wife, he has never attempted to do anything to me!!!

During the year, he started noticing students on campus wearing New World Order T-shirts, and even caught various students conversing with each other during their breaks, usually outside about how great a thing the New World Order was and how they planned to make it come to pass sooner than it might have come. God is in control not these students. They could not have done such a thing. God allows these things to come to pass in his timing not theirs.

He also noticed two or three of his other classmates having this very same conversation.

He also had problems with the girls at this college acting funny about him and making bizarre comments about him, and some of them acted like they thought he was hiding something. He finally got tired of it and told them he wasn't hiding anything.

Because they bugged him so much about this, he did tell them he liked women's feet and that he'd like to play footsy with whoever would like to be his girlfriend. He thought they'd never leave him alone, so, he finally told them this and it got him in trouble. He wrote a girl about this and tried to defend himself as to what others thought of him at the same time, and he still got in trouble. He also asked girls he was interested in if this would be a problem with them, so that he could avoid any hard feelings from them.

You see, when he went to High School, he went to a slumber party at a neighbor friend's house, and it was him, his friend, his friend's brother, his sister, and his sister's girlfriend that was there. His friend's sister begged him to take his socks off. (Brian is very shy about his feet.) She finally talked him into it. His friend's sister's girlfriend played blindfold with him and kept choosing him on purpose. Then all four of them went into the bedroom and set at the head of the bed to watch a movie. Next thing he knew, the girl next to him that was the sister's girlfriend, who was also barefooted, started rubbing her feet against his and he liked it. Someone informed him later on that this was called footsy. Ever since this girl did this, he wanted to do this again with the very next girl that would be his girlfriend. And every chance he got, which was very seldom, when he actually got a girl for a while, that's exactly what he did, and that's the way he wanted it ever since. He did this with me, as well when we started dating, even on the first week we dated. I was so confused, it made me extremely excited. Brian just got pleasure out of it like a massage. I thought, He has to be gay for this not to excite him. He didn't know anything about sex yet. He was so cute, and innocent like a child.

Back to the 1994 experience, before he got a job at the hospital outside of town August 8, 1994-August 18, 1995, that Spring, he had previously applied for a job at the main hospital in town, and there were two ladies that appeared only slightly older than him, walking toward the hospital in the lane his car was parked, which was a long ways down that lane. When they saw him coming they acted like they thought he was after them or something, and he hadn't done anything to them. He didn't even say anything to them. He was just walking to his car, and these two ladies acted like they thought he was suspicious and gave him the weirdest look when they walked past him, and he thought, Cant I walk to my own car? Brian doesn't realize he has a very domineering walk because of his Autism. Not knowing this made them very uncomfortable but they shouldn't have reacted that way to him.

One time at the college he went to in the Summer of 1991, there was a lady he was kind of interested in then, and it was semester exam day, and he thought, I've got to act fast if I'm going to get this one to go with me, so he wrote her a note and asked her if she'd be his girlfriend. Believe it or not, this time it was only one page, when he writes its never one page. He has to give every detail. At the end of class her, and a couple of students stood at the desk having a conversation about wife beaters and he waited for a minute, but he had a leery feeling about it. He finally walked out the door to got to his car, and she ran into the lobby out in front of him and started walking the same way, and tried to make it appear as if he was following her, but he kept on walking, and by the time he got to the front door, she ran back to the classroom making it look like she was afraid of him and that she was trying to get away, but he walked the rest of the way to his car, and didn't go back He thought, What on earth was that all about, anyway. That lady's weird.

There were times at college that he would say things that the students would twist around into what they wanted him to say. They believed that every word that came out of a person's mouth was symbolic, that nothing anybody ever said could be taken literally, especially if it was some one like him that didn't necessarily talk like they did. Because of his low voice, when he would say things they would judge him for having evil intentions for not phrasing things the politically correct way, or if Brian didn't phrase it the way they thought a statement should be phrased. What difference does it make if there is two or three different ways a person can phrase a statement and mean the same thing. He told his mother about this and she thought the colleges were making these students take too many English Literature classes and that this was messing up their head about what everything meant.

Most of the bad experiences he had were at a college, but occasionally he'd run into a situation like this one in 1994 out in the community where he didn't know what was going on. This is how they'd react to him, and he'd think, What did I do? I didn't do anything. What's the problem anyway? Doesn't anybody trust me anymore? He thinks they prejudged him for his funny body language, as did the college students. He's not for sure, if he had to guess he'd highly suspect it. There was a lot of New Ageism in Abilene. That's the way people think down there.

Since he moved to Berryville, Arkansas he's never had this problem again. He thought he was safe until he met the Director of Speech Pathology of this hospital two hours away from Berryville. Then everything broke loose everywhere because he was scared to death that the nightmare he had in Abilene was about to come to life.

Speech Pathology Department Incident

    We were looking for a language therapist to go to at this hospital hoping they could help him better communicate with his doctors and nurses. He talked to a therapist there on the phone three times. Brian explained his disability to her, I should have done this but we didn't know about his Autism yet. Brian tried to explain to her the things he had problems with (communicative-wise) that the Speech and Hearing Center at a college in Texas worked on. Brian said he'd like her to do the same thing and see how much further he could get. Brian is very persistent. That's why he kept calling. He did admit that he wasn't too bad off anymore and that it was very hard to tell that he even had a communication problem because it was so hard to detect. Most of the time he communicates real well, but sometimes he gets in sticky situations and doesn't know what to say or how to handle things. Sometimes he has days where either he'd blank out on everybody, or he'd try to tell you something and you wonder what on earth he's talking about. Just try to have a two way conversation with him. How are you today? He would say fine and that's it! Now when the subject is very important to him like the IV helper situation he doesn't ever shut up! I even had to find some medicine to help with all his anxiety over the whole thing. I was fixing to lose my mind! It was the same thing over and over, man I couldn't take it anymore. There are times when he says something and it makes sense to him, but it doesn't make since to anyone else. She finally told him she was an in-patient therapist, and that he would have to talk to somebody at the building across from the hospital. He had a horrible time getting their phone number from the other staff, but finally got it. They acted almost as if they didn't want to give it to him for some reason. Brian has a very domineering personality when he wants something because of his Autism. They probably didn't want him to bug them. I wish I would have known what I know now. I could have saved him from this awful experience!

He called the secretary at the other building and asked, who they had that could give him therapy and she said there was a lady and a man. For some reason, he already had a bad feeling about both of them. He asked if he could have the lady therapist, and she acted funny about it, like she thought something bad about his request and said, It depends on their schedule. You'll get one or the other and you'll never know which one. It will be which ever one is available, and which one whose schedule you fit into the best. They were probably fore-warned by the office staff across the street. Brian can sound really smart on the phone. This is a perfect example of how Autistic people have a very hard time getting their point across. Brian should have just forgotten about it as soon as he had the bad feeling. I think it must have been the Holy Spirit telling him not to go there. But Brian is not very good at picking up on what is a bad feeling and what is the Holy Spirit trying to have him go a different way. Hind-site is twenty-twenty, but this would have sure saved us a lot of troubles with his favorite IV-helper!

I decided to go to the building of the speech therapist with him when we went to the Urologist on January 3, 2005. I thought it would put an end to any misconceptions about him wanting a female therapist if his wife was with him. Brian wanted to meet the therapists to see which one he would be more comfortable with. We saw the secretary there, I asked, Can we meet the therapists? The lady gave us a hard time, but we finally got through what we wanted. Brian asked her if he could have a lady therapist, and told her he preferred the inpatient lady therapist he talked to on the phone, but if not he wanted the lady outpatient therapist and not the man! I should have explained why he wanted the female. If I just would have straightened it out then and there none of this would have happened. Once again hindsight is 20/20! But we learn from our mistakes. We can become bitter or better! I pray I am a better wife/advocate for Brian. I wish he wouldn't have had to go through so much turmoil just so I could learn my duties as a wife of an Autistic man.

She acted funny again and said that the lady therapist he talked to on the phone was an in."
patient therapist, so it would probably be either the lady or the man in the outpatient therapy department. She told me she'd leave the therapists a note and they'd check their schedule to see when they could meet with us.

The next day, I called the outpatient lady therapist's number and left a message for her to call back so I could explain him to her. I decided to go to the Free Store for a couple of hours to go through donations. Instead of the lady therapist calling, the Director of Speech Pathology called. This director spoke very abrasively to Brian on the phone and introduced himself in a sarcastic tone of voice, and then he said, I have here a note that you would like to meet with my Speech Pathologists! My Speech Pathologists cannot meet with you! I keep them busy and they Don't have time to talk to you, so I suggest you call back in June when you get your prescription and contact us then! Then, we can go from there! (In a very domineering, abrasive, dictatorial voice yelling) Once again I wasn't there when Brian needed me. If I had been there I may have said the wrong thing out of anger. God knows what He is doing! All things work out for the good of those who love the Lord!

After the way the director of speech pathology and his secretary acted, Brian immediately felt that he had to defend himself to these Speech Pathologists, so he decided to write the outpatient lady therapist a letter explaining why he wanted a female therapist and why it meant so much to him and he began explaining his childhood to her and how it impacted his future in the way he thought. He told her about bad experiences in his past where he was harassed by different male figures including teachers and peers and how he always went to the female teachers and female peers for comfort because he was constantly bullied. He also told her about an experience he had with two lab men in the hospital making fun of him for his fear of needles and how they rammed the needle in as hard as they could to make themselves feel big and laughed when he screamed about it. He would say, Are you almost done yet? They'd just laugh and say, No! We have a long way to go! When they were done, they'd say, Maybe You'll do better the next time! The whole time they'd make comments like Do we have a baby in here?! I think we have a baby in here! We're going to have to make a man out of this guy! Not only is he oversensitive to pain, but also his doctor's wife said she thinks he was traumatized by this experience and this has only made the problem worse. When Brian writes as you learned in the last chapter you get every detail of his past more often than not over and over. After explaining these things to the outpatient lady therapist, he also included 2 pages worth of language and autism problems, one page about autistic tendencies and one page about language disorders.

He also explained to the out-patient lady therapist that he had 6 female clinicians at a college in Texas before he even moved up here and said that he didn't understand why everybody was so huffy about his asking for a lady therapist, for because he had 6 (one at a time, a semester a piece) before he moved up here and they were totally fine with him. He asked her to please try to understand him and give him a chance. He told her in his letter if this made her uncomfortable to be his therapist because he was a man to please write him back and let him know and he'd go elsewhere and find someone else that would be willing to be his female therapist.

He wrote a letter identical to this one to the secretary as well, because she's the one that acted so weird about everything in the first place and he also told her he couldn't understand what everyone was so huffy about because he had 6 female therapists before them and they were totally fine with him.

Next, he wrote a letter to the in-patient therapist asking her if there was any way she could make an exception and be his outpatient therapist and suggested to her if she thought it would work, he could go above the director's head to the boss above him to see if he could get it approved. I wish I could have stopped him before this comment. It's not a good thing to say you will go over somebody's head. He was getting very desperate. He also tried to explain what kind of therapist/patient relationship he wanted to have, and begged her not to get the wrong idea. He wanted her to hug him and let him hug her when he saw her, and he also begged her to let him cry on her shoulder if he was mistreated by another person, or if a friend or relative died, or a traumatic experience took place. Brian doesn't realize this is what a wife is for. At this time in our marriage I don't think I would have done these things very well. I didn't know about his Autism yet. What he did not think to explain was that his 6 ex-clinicians (speech-language therapists) always gave him a hug and patted him on the shoulder when he first saw them to make him feel good about going to therapy and he did the same thing with them, and this is what he was used to. He also failed to make it clear that when he said he wanted it to be like a student and a favorite teacher, he was referring to the way he was treated by his Special Ed teachers in the 7th grade before he went into regular classes the next year. He just looks like a man. He still has the needs of a child. He had a favorite teacher in the 7th grade he really liked and she really liked him, too. This lady sort of reminded him of her when he was on the phone and he wanted her to be like this lady was with him. This is something else he did not clearly explain. This is why he wanted her so bad, she acted like she understood him and it would be like living the 7th grade all over again if she was his therapist, especially since he found two operating room nurses he really liked that also reminded him of his 7th grade special ed English teacher, particularly the IV helper. These two people also reminded him of a couple at church he went wild over every time he saw them.

    This is why they also meant so much to him, because they acted so much like them and they were the first two people to ever get him successfully through an IV stick and still be friendly afterwards. They started out pumping him up like a best friend and then acted like a kind mother helping talk him through a procedure with soft comforting words, showing affection, and giving him oxygen as well, to help him get through it. It really helped a lot. Most people get mad at him and quit after they've barely even started.

Brian was panicked and suggested different wrong things the in-patient therapist might say, think, or do in the letter he wrote because he was afraid the Director of the Speech Pathology Department was going to try to make her think he was just after the women, that he didn't really need therapy because he couldn't see the problem right off the bat.

The Director of the Speech Pathology Department called back about four days after he sent the letters to his therapists. This director spoke abrasively again and said, I have here letters to several of my therapists! I would like to ask that you not write or call my therapists! Could you do that for me? You can contact us in June when you get your prescription, and, by the way your therapist will be Dan when you come because the Director of Speech Pathology thought he was after the women, he got worried, and thought, Oh no! What if he gets to my favorite IV helper?

He got all wound up and wrote the letter to the IV sticker that should have been addressed to the IV helper. He began begging them not to say all those strange comments to him that he made all because he was afraid the IV helper would begin to act like the people in Abilene because of this director. He is very sorry he said these things because he was panicked. He begged the IV sticker to let his favorite IV helper nurse be her assistant again, and got wound up with them, too because he was afraid they'd get the wrong idea about his being so chummy with them (acting overly excited to see them) and start acting funny because they might think he liked them too much. He begged them not to feel this way, no matter how glad he was to see them. He did not explain however, that this was the way people did with him in Special Ed, You pump me up! I pump you up! You pump me up again! The people in regular classes, especially the girls in high school and college did not understand this concept with the exception of a few people and, this was the part he told them about. He also told them about being upset about doctors not taking his medical problems seriously enough to find the real problems, for example, the heart defects found on him at age 6 years and 9 months that doctors refuse to believe he has because he is not yet 50-years-old.

This is also true for the prostate surgery he just had, all the doctors he went to in Arkansas did not believe him, except for one regardless of past evidence from records when he was in his 20s because he was not yet 50-years-old. He also suggested different things he was afraid they would think because of the way the Director of Speech Pathology acted and begged them not to say, think, or do those things, but be his friend anyway. Some of the comments he made that may have been misunderstood were comments he repeated that some college girls in Abilene said to him that he put in their mouth out of fear these would be things they said if the director turned them against him and they are as follows: I'm not your mother! I'm not your girlfriend! I'm not your hero! was a comment made by a girl in Abilene that Brian tried to make friends with when he was at college. He didn't know why she made this comment because he had not asked for any favors from her. He was just trying to be her friend. Because of the situation with the Director of Speech Pathology Brian was afraid his favorite IV helper would make the same comment when he tried to be her friend. He was worried later she might think that he was trying to get her to be a girlfriend when he stated this, but this was not the reason for the comment. He was simply repeating something somebody else said in his past, and, he was afraid that if he sought this IV helper for comfort, especially if he asked her to rub his head to calm him down after an IV stick, she might say, I'm not your mother! What do you want from me anyway! She never gave him an indication to think this about her, he was just afraid she would begin to act like this if the director turned her against him. 2. Why do you like me so much? This was a comment made by a girl that got the wrong idea after he acted pumped to see her for the 3rd or 4th time, but the girl had really encouraged it in the beginning, so she should have expected that kind of reaction from Brian. He was afraid his IV helper would think he was up to no good if he acted excited to see her a 3rd or 4th times in a row and wouldn't understand him anymore because of what the director might tell her to turn her against him 3. About the thing where he was afraid his own church would turn against him, there was really no reason to fear this because he got along with his church peers great. He was just afraid if he tried to be buddies with the children's church group leaders that they might not understand why he was so wound up over them, but they did understand and they've been buddies ever since. 4. There was a kid that acted like the college girl in comment #2, that Brian felt this little girl made because she thought he was dumb for getting that excited to see her. She really brought it on herself, because she encouraged him to act like that to start with and then, later wondered why he still did. This is highly unusual, because most kids love Brian to death. Her parents told Brian that she does that to all her friends and when she gets a new one she dumps the old one.

About the comment he made about trying to get his IV helper to rub his head, he meant no harm by this and did not mean to offend the lady. Because of his Autism he has special needs that most people don't have and this is one of them. This is what he needs this nurse to do to calm him down when he's crying and hyperventilating over the IV stick he just had.

About 4 days after Brian wrote this letter, the police called and said, I'd like to ask that you not write or call anybody in the hospital. Can you do this for me? Brian told him yes, but he did not say we could not go in there. I had no idea he was writing the hospital. I would come home from volunteering at the Free Store and there would be a note saying, Went to the post office. Be right back. I never imagined he would be doing anything wrong, so I didn't even think twice.

We asked a policeman we knew in town if I could go and explain my Husband's conditions to all these people, particularly the IV helper. Brian was worried it was because he wrote about her that he was in trouble. He highly suspected that the Speech Pathology Department was behind this. The policeman we knew in town thought this would be okay.

When we went for Brian's appointment on January 13, 2005, he was worried about the letter he sent to the IV sticker nurse that was mainly aimed at the IV helper. He begged the IV sticker nurse to use the same IV helper nurse again and begged them not, to say, think, or do any of the things the Abilene people did, but did not explain this is where he got it from.

He wanted to talk to the IV helper because he was afraid she might have mistook the letter, so we went up to the hospital and I asked to speak to her. We were given the extension line, and I talked to her for a minute, but the IV helper said I'd have to be quick because she only had a minute to talk to me in the waiting room. I said that was okay. The IV helper then told me she got off at 2:30 pm, and since it was 2:00 pm, we assumed if we waited, she'd come and talk to us.

By 2:20 pm, here came a policeman and said, What are you doing here?! We told him we came to talk to Brian's favorite IV helper, and he said, No, but, Why did you come here? You drove 2 hours to come up here just to talk to her? Why are you here? I explained it to the officer again, but he wouldn't listen. He acted like he didn't believe that's why we were there. Has someone upset you? Are you mad at somebody?! Why are you here?! He then frisked Brian in the hallway and said, I get a little nervous about things like this. He acted like he thought Brian had a gun, but he didn't find one because he didn't have one. Brian doesn't like guns they make him very uncomfortable. Because of this fact, you will never find one on him.

Brian's eyes were huge! He didn't know what in the world was going on. He was very cordial. He did everything just as the officer directed. I know he must have thought they were taking him to jail. I was so scared. I didn't know what to do! I had no idea what was written in any of the letters, or, how many of them he had written. Brian offered to go over the content of the letters with him, but the officer said, Oh no! I'm not even going to go over the content! I'm glad the officer did not discuss what was in the letters because I would not have been able to stick up for him because I had no idea what was in them. Brian is very innocent, he wrote things that could have been taken either way depending on the mindset of the reader. He has no reasoning skills that would have helped him to write in a way that would not have been taken wrong. If he would have thought to have me proofread the letters, I would have been able to pick out and change the parts that were taken wrong. The officer said the hospital had a stack of letters 14 inches thick that he had written to several people.

There have been murderers who did the exact same thing, so the hospital was trying to protect its employees. If they just would have read one of the letters, they would have figured out he was not a criminal. I wish we would have known before all this happened that he was Autistic. We told the officer he had Autistic tendencies but he said, The law Doesn't recognize disabilities.

I know the reason the stack was so thick. Brian is a detail person and I was sure after he told me what was in them that he told each person he wrote to every single detail of his whole life. Brian is Autistic and autistic people are not able to communicate like you and I. His method of communication is writing. Being autistic, he is very detailed. He doesn't want any one to miss anything.

The officer took Brian downstairs and had him talk to two other policeman. They were all deputies. I told Brian to let me do the talking. He would never listen to Brian or I because he had his own idea of what was going on. Brian told him, I know a policeman in Berryville that knows what kind of person I am and I could have him explain me to you. He just said, It won't be necessary. He didn't need to talk to him.

He told us we were asked not to come to the hospital on the phone. I reminded him that he said no such thing, he only said that Brian Couldn't write or call the people at the hospital again which he hadn't done. The officer just wanted to believe Brian was evil. The officer said that since Brian was concerned about which nurse he would get that his doctor could talk to them about it. Only the doctor could say who would be his nurse. Brian told the doctor what happened, but he just didn't understand just like he didn't understand Brian's fear of needles. Brian found out later that the doctor thought he was stalking his favorite IV helper. He wasn't, he was just begging for mercy. After the officer was done getting on to us, he showed us a shortcut out of the hospital. He wouldn't let us go talk to anybody. After this incident my life was a living disaster. Over and over he would talk about this IV helper. I got so tired of hearing it! I wanted to pray for her death just so he would shut up about having her be his nurse every time but "vengence is mine", saith the Lord! I always get what I pray for too so I would have felt like a murderer if I even knew it happened.

In August before this happened we found out that Brian's social security disability records had indicated Brian had autistic tendencies. We had saved up money to have Brian tested. Finally, he saved enough in December, and the soonest appointment was January 19th.

The psychologist told us it would take three, one-hour sessions to diagnose Brian. When we went to his appointment we took all of his childhood records and every piece of information we could find on his childhood. The psychologist told us it was so obvious from the records and the things we told her about the present that we didn't need to come back. She made the diagnosis immediately. So, instead of $425, we only had to pay $175 for the testing. The psychologist wondered why on earth someone didn't diagnose him a long time ago when he was a child.

His mother knew his behavior matched perfectly with an Autistic child. When she asked to have him tested they told her he is too old. People do not grow out of Autism! If you are autistic you are always autistic!

His diagnosis was Autism, active. He also has a personality disorder, an anxiety disorder, ulcers, and prostate-problems, just to name a few. While we were at it, I told this psychologist that Brian was oversensitive to pain and he couldn't help it that he reacted so adversely to people sticking him with IVs, blood tests, catheters, etc. and she told us about Emla (Lidocaine) and suggested he put it on the site they plan to do the stick one hour before they put in an IV so it will numb the arm and make it hurt less than it would have. Ever since we found this out, even though Brian still screamed and cried a lot, he has actually done a whole lot better since he started using this Lidocaine before getting stuck for procedures.

At this time, Brian had to go to the Urologist about every 2 weeks. The urologist said his problem was an overactive sphincter. He thought it would get fixed since he made an incision in it. It didn't work. He said he couldn't do a sphincterectomy because Brian would be incontinent and urinate all over himself.

He didn't know what to do. He kept having pencil lead thin streams and occasional dribbling. He thought the Urologist needed to do something, but he never would. The urologist did say, however, he was eventually going to have to go in there to see what was going on.

After almost 6 months of this, the Urologist decided to put Brian in the hospital. He was going to do a dilatation (dilation) the second to the last week of May. His Medicare did not start until June 1st, so the Urologist made him wait until June 7th. That was the soonest time he could see him after he received Medicare. The Urologist's nurse claimed to have talked to the IV helper in Pre-op to get him set up with her, but insisted he would go to the GI department instead of pre-op. The Urologist's nurse said she talked to his favorite IV helper and she had told her, If at all possible, if I'm working that day, I will be his IV helper. If not, the lady in the GI department would do it. When he got there he was supposed to ask for his favorite IV helper. When he did, they claimed they hadn't heard anything about his favorite IV helper coming over there to help him. They finally called her and they claimed she said she couldn't because she was too busy with other patients.

Because of this, Brian was upset for not insisting on Pre-op. He figured the nurse he wanted wasn't going to come clear to GI to help him.

When they took him to a room, I noticed a security guard following us everywhere. He stood outside of the room Brian was in.

After this they said Brian could change into his gown, but if he was too embarrassed he could wait a few minutes. Brian thinks they said this because of one of the letters talking about how nurses humiliated him.

He changed, and after several minutes this boring IV nurse came in to do his IV. She was not near as good as his original IV sticker. She even had to stick him twice to get the IV in the right spot. He reached out for her hand, and after a minute or two, she said, Now, let go of my hand. Okay.

He screamed very loudly and another nurse in the GI department said, You're going to have to go ahead and put him in the Cysto suite! I can't take anymore of this screaming! He's scaring the other patients!

It was a few minutes before they did. I talked to the IV nurse out in the hall and said, Your going to have to put him out! He can't be awake or he'll freak out! The nurse said, He's going to be a little woozy. He won't be completely knocked out. I said again, You're going to have to put him out! You can't let him be awake! He's going to freak out! I told her this again. Then I said, I'm telling you! He's going to freak out if you don't! I was afraid this nurse would not cooperate, but, thank you God, when she got finished arguing with me, she said she would knock him out.

They finally took Brian in the Cysto Suite and the security guard followed him in there. Brian looked at him like he was worried he'd have to do everything awake. The doctor finally came in, and Brian said, Your going to have to put me completely out! I can't handle it if you don't! The doctor said, Okay, I'll have them put a little something in your IV. The doctor and the IV nurse looked at the Security Guard and said, We won't be needing you in here. Before Brian even went in the Cysto Suite he saw the security guard in the hallway and eventually another man went in the hall and started talking to him who Brian assumed must have been the Administrator. This security guard actually acted like he thought this whole thing was ridiculous and wondered why he was even there. He went along with it and never said anything. After his dilatation (dilation) was over; the Security Guard, the doctor and the IV nurse all 3 wheel-chaired him to the car. At one point, I saw three policemen hanging out in the hallway. I was glad Brian didn't see them. After this experience I told Brian I never wanted to go back to this hospital again! I didn't like the way they treated him like he was a criminal.

In July of 2005, he wrote his favorite IV nurse and sent the letter to a relative's house so she'd get it, because he didn't know her exact address. He is a concrete thinker, so in doing this, he was not disobeying the officer, because it wasn't to the hospital and it wasn't a phone call.

He asked her if something was still wrong because he understood everything was okay now. He was confused after the situation with the security guard and the police. He tried desperately to explain why he did what he did when he wrote the letter he had written to her boss pertaining to her. He feared he was horribly mistaken and tried to defend himself. He begged her to be his nurse again and told her how scared he was of some nurses. It was very important that she be the one because she was the type of nurse he liked and the type of nurse he was comfortable with. He begged her to give him a second chance. He wrote a thirteen, page letter and 5 postcards to plea with her for mercy and another chance. She didn't understand, so, she called the police.

The police station in her county called and said, You were asked not to write this lady again, or speak to her again. Do not write her. Do not call her. Do not go to see her at the hospital. Don't have any contact with her. She doesn't want to have anything to do with you. If you write her again, I'm going to have to take you in for stalking. Do you understand? Okay. Don't have any contact with her or you'll be taken in. Around the same time, he wrote his doctor complaining to his doctor about his treatment at the hospital. He insisted that he be treated with respect and not like a criminal. He also suggested alternative ways this nurse could punish him just in order to get her to talk to him and assure her at the same time she was safe. When he got through, he eventually got a letter from the doctor's office stating his letter was offensive, and the wife of the doctor insisted he cease this correspondence immediately. From now on, they were going to schedule Brian to be seen when there were no other patients scheduled because he caused too many distractions.

He would hug everybody regardless of whether or not they were attending to a patient. He's just sweet that way. I took this letter to say basically, Your no longer welcome here. There was never a time when his office was empty, so Brian would never get scheduled.

He was still having a lot of problems going to the bathroom. One Urologist's office almost took him after I explained the reason for what happened. The doctor of that clinic said he couldn't take him because of the stalking letters. All the other Urologists besides him refused right away. It took this Urologist a week or two before he said, NO. He decided not to take Brian right after they received records from this Urologist. Brian wrote those letters in panic because of a past experience similar to the one he currently faced. It freaked him out, and even though he didn't make it clear what he was talking about, he just didn't want his IV nurse to act like the people in Abilene did before he moved up here. The comments he made were simply repeats of what the Abilene people said, which he frantically put in his IV sticker's and IV helper's mouth in fear they would be the same way. If it were not for the experience he had in the Speech Pathology department that scared him, he would have never written the letters in the first place.

Soon afterwards, his Family Doctor set him up with a doctor to perform a colonoscopy due to the hard, dull pains in the stomach that were tight and stretched. Brian was having multiple bowel movements.

I explained Brian to this doctor. He set him up with a lady Urologist who eventually set him up with her husband, the other Urologist in the same office. This doctor said, In this case, you need to give him a little more slack. He just needs to find a circle of doctors who understand his Autism and surround him with them.

I took him to this lady Urologist and she set Brian up with her husband to do a Cystoscopy and then an Urodynamics study. She was very nice and liked Brian very much. Her husband was the nicest doctor I have ever known and he liked Brian, too. When Brian went for his colonoscopy he asked me to tell the doctor's nurse to see to it that he got all happy go lucky nurses. They all needed to be female, because Brian is very uncomfortable with men nurses. He said, He particularly needed the IV person to be happy go lucky. They needed another IV helper that was very happy go lucky to hold his hand and rub the top of his head to calm him down.

Come to find out, all his nurses were female, but the person doing the IV was a guy. This made Brian very nervous, however, he told the guy how scared he was. He said because of Brian's autism they were going to go ahead and do the gas first and put the IV in when he is already asleep. This made Brian very happy! He got to see all 5 of his pre-op nurses and his 2 favorite ones got to stand next to where his head was and they were all lined up from head to foot. I asked when Brian got there if he could have the same people every time, and, from what I understood, it's set. He should get the same ones every time.

When the test was over, the doctor told Brian he had a stretched out colon (large intestine) and his stomach and colon were both very inflamed. Everything was normal and no major diseases were present.

When Brian went to his new Urologist in September 2005 he did bladder scopes on him and they read that Brian held 600-900 ml of urine after voiding (urinating in the bathroom). This was very abnormal and we tried to find the cause. The Urologist before this Urologist would not do bladder scopes on Brian even though he asked him to. He insisted on just doing bladder pressure tests which were okay and probably were important, but he should have done bladder scopes every visit like this Urologist did so he could see what level of retention Brian had which showed he retained way too much urine. This Urologist did bladder scopes on every visit Brian made to the doctor's office and it showed him what the other Urologist really needed to see. If this Urologist Brian previously had would have done the bladder scopes on Brian when he went for his appointments, he would have seen for himself how bad it was and took Brian much more seriously after taking this test every time.

At first the Urologist did a Cystoscope to check for prostate blockage, but claimed Brian was wide open yet admitted he still had a problem. He had put Brian in the hospital for a day with a catheter in him to get the flow readjusted. He decided he wanted to do an Urodynamics x-ray the next week and this was frightening to Brian. He told Brian, I'm not going to do anything to try to hurt you, but I really think we need to do this to find out what's wrong.

Just as the doctor expected, the bladder had almost quit working completely. When Brian started to void according to the test, the bladder just sat there and didn't do anything, and the test also indicated he had an overactive sphincter on top of this which made things worse. The doctor put Brian on Bethenecol to force the bladder to work. The lower dose quit working, so he raised it to the higher dose, but Brian still had problems.

On October 31, 2005 he performed an operation to put a pubic catheter in and had made Brian wear a catheter all the way to January 10th, 2006. When it felt like urine was trying to come out, that doctor decided to plug it for a week when we went for our appointment on January 3rd to test it. On January 10th, he removed the catheter and gave Brian the maximum dose of Bethenecol. He did better for a week or two then things were shaky until about March. By April or May Brian finally went normal most of the time. From June on it's gone from better to worse to better to worse. Right now he's having a downslide where he'll dribble or have a narrow stream during the afternoon, then it lets up for 2 or 3 days, then, he'll have another bad afternoon. It's still not near as bad as it was the first time, but Brian feels like he's having prostate problems again and may or may not have to have another TURP at some future date if it doesn't clear up or gets worse.

When Brian went to the Pre-op for his procedures at this hospital, we told the nurses he wanted all happy go lucky nurses for his in-patient nurses and he wanted the same ones every time and they put this in his record and he got the same ones both times that he was in in-patient care. I also told them Brian wanted a happy go lucky female nurse to help him with his IV and he picked the person that helped him and the one he wanted to do the stick and he got what he wanted. They also put in his record that he needed hugs from all his nurses and he got them, and he got along great with all of them.

The one time Brian had to go for an Urodynamics at the hospital they shot lidocaine in him before inserting the catheter, but he still screamed and cried in pain. When Brian has a catheter stuck in him awake it feels like someone just stuck a sword in him. It takes a special person to be able to get Brian through something like this and even they might be lucky if they get him through it. This real nice lady nurse inserted the catheter while the doctor held his hand and tried to keep him distracted to get him through the painful experience. Brian recently asked this lady to be his IV helper the next time he went into the hospital instead of the one he originally chose and she said, Sure! The doctor tried to get Brian to talk about things he liked and things he liked to do with his time and this lady nurse kept asking him the same kind of questions. The doctor also tried to keep him humored to get his mind off the catheter. It still hurt with excruciating pain.

Regardless of the better set up situation at this hospital however, Brian would really prefer the nurse at the other hospital that was his favorite IV helper to be his IV helper for all his procedures if he can just get her to forgive him for the delirious letter he wrote to her boss and give him a second chance. This nurse is very special to Brian and he wants her to be his nurse more than anybody else in the world. Brian hopes that she sees all this and sees how he was handled at the other hospitals he's been to and realize he meant her no harm. He hopes that one day she'll be his nurse again and he and everyone else will be very happy again.

Brian can't get the fact that if he had a doctor in Berryville or Harrison, they are not going to send him to where she is. I'm praying that God moves her to Berryville or Harrison. When He does the other nurses will straighten her out. They all love Brian. They think of him as a loveable little boy, that is exactly what he is.

I just recently had a hysterectomy at a different hospital that we've never been to before, and the nurses there all gave Brian hugs and cheered him on after they saw in my record that I stated I had an Autistic husband that needs hugs from all the nurses. All of them, including my Pre-op nurse liked him and gave him hugs. If we ever have to go to this hospital again, Brian is hoping if he is the one that has to go that the same lady nurse that did my IV does his IV as well, because this is who he would be comfortable with doing it at this hospital.

When it comes to situations like the hospital incident where Brian got in trouble with his favorite IV nurse at the first hospital I spoke about, it's better to console him and reassure him that none of the things he mentions he's afraid of happening is ever going to happen and everything's okay. If this nurse would have done this and then promised Brian she would be his nurse from now on, like these other nurses did for him, then he'd be fine and never give her a problem about it again and we could go on as usual as if the whole thing never happened. This is another example of his autism not allowing him to grasp reality. She couldn't possibly be the one every-time. She can't go to where Brian is having a procedure done. Her boss wouldn't pay her to do this.

Brian only says the types of things he said to his favorite IV helper because, somebody else has picked on him. This has caused him to fear about things that probably would have never happened.

Brian used to do this exact same thing with his elementary school Special Ed teachers when another boy or another male teacher tried to make him think they were going to turn everyone against him. When he did this, they knew this had to be what the deal was and they'd console Brian on the spot and assure him that none of the things he feared would ever happen and assure him that they were still friends. When they did this, Brian was okay.

Brian would like to write a script of how he would like his favorite IV helper at the first hospital to respond to him and handle him. Here it goes:

Brian: (Runs up to his favorite IV helper to give her a hug and very excitedly calls her name)
IV helper: (Encourages him in a robust tone of voice) We're going to get through this! Don't you worry! You're going to make it! We're going to get you through this and your going to be okay!
Brian: (Appalled) You really think you can get someone like me through an IV?
IV helper: (With excitement, robust tone of voice) Yes! You're going to be just fine! Don't you worry! We're going to get you through this! We're going to take care of you! You'll be just fine! You'll see!
Brian: (With surprise) Thank you. I hope I do all-right.
IV helper: You're going to be fine! IV helper: Come on! Let's go back here and I'll show you where to go!
IV helper: (Takes me to the Patient Room, hands me my gown, and, tells me to change and let her know when I'm ready)
IV helper: Let me know when you're ready.(Waits outside curtain)
Brian: Okay!
IV helper: You ready!
Brian: Yeah.
IV helper: Now lay down here and the other nurse is going to be here in a minute to start your IV. IV sticker: I'm just looking for a spot!
Brian: (In fear looks at the IV sticker and then the IV helper)
IV Sticker: Now turn around and look at the IV helper and hold her hand, and, I'm going to stick it in right now!
IV helper: (Holds my hand)
Brian: (Crying, Hyperventilating, Hysterical in Pain)

IV sticker: Let me give you the oxygen. This should help a little bit.
IV Helper: (Seeing I'm still hysterical, crying, hyperventilating, etc. reaches over and rubs my head to calm me down) Sh… Shh It's going to be all right. You're going to be okay. We're going to make it, okay. Just bear with me. You're going to be okay. It's going to be all right
IV helper: (Stands there waiting for the gas people to come and comforts me at the same time by rubbing my head to calm me down while she's waiting,) The gas person walks in the room.
Brian: (To the IV helper) I want a goodbye hug before you go.
IV Helper: (Gives Brian a goodbye hug to make him feel better and wishes him luck) The gas person rides me off and I wave at my favorite IV helper as they take me off. When they bring me back form surgery, if my IV helper is still there, I give her another goodbye hug once again, and we all say goodbye and I go home. If I have to stay a few days in the hospital, I get a goodbye hug. We say goodbye. And, I go to the Inpatient Care Room. After my time is over, say 3 to 5 days for example, I go back and say my final goodbyes to my IV helper and hug her again. Occasionally, I'd like to visit her, and give her a hug and say, Hi, and I'll try not to do it too often, maybe once every two or three months like I do all my other nurses at all the other hospitals I go to, and hope she's in good spirits to see me. Is that all that bad? Is that so much to ask? That's all I ask. End of Script

Now Brian would like to tell you a story in cartoon form to show you how his situation with his favorite IV nurse makes him feel. Here it goes.

Have you ever seen the kid show about Barney the purple dinosaur?

There was one episode where Barney played doctor with a kid to make them feel better about going to see the doctor, and the kid loved Barney! To the kid's surprise, when they went to see the doctor for real the second time they found out that Barney was the doctor, and said, Barney! It's you! You're the doctor! with great excitement. Then Barney said, Yes! It's me! Are you glad to be here now?! The kid says, Yes! After a while Barney told the kid that he'd have to give him a shot, but he did it in such a way that was so nice in the way he gave the shot to the kid that it made it not so bad that the kid had to get a shot. This made the kid very happy.

Let's suppose however, that after this kid so loved and cherished having Barney for their doctor, that an evil man came along and tried to ruin their relationship with Barney. The evil man has the wrong idea about the kid, and, says, I'm going to tell Barney that you're not really as bad off as you say you are when you claim to be sick and that you are just going to Barney to get by with something because you have evil intentions and he's going to believe me! See what you think of your Barney now! He'll never be your friend again because I'll convince him that you're really bad! Try getting your Barney back now! He'll never like you again because when I get through with him, he'll think you're really bad! The kid goes and speaks to Barney in dismay, No! Barney it's not true! He's lying to you! You've got to believe me! Please! Barney in anger says, Don't speak to me! Don't ever speak to me again! I never want to see you again! Go home and never come back! The kid pleads with Barney and says, Barney! Please! Don't do this! Don't do this to me! It's not true! It's not really the way he says! He's lying to you! You've got to believe me! Please! The kid goes away severely depressed and never is the same again because he feels like he's lost his Barney forever and never will be happy again until the day his relationship with Barney is restored.

You see, you know how kids are toward Barney the purple dinosaur. The way kids feel about Barney is the same way Brian feels about his IV helper. Just as this kid got his feelings hurt severely when Barney rejected him, so Brian got his feelings hurt in the same way the kid did about Barney. Brian's favorite IV helper is Barney in this cartoon, and the Director of Speech Pathology is the evil man who may have tried to turn her against him forever because of his false belief that Brian had evil intentions for wanting to have her for his nurse. Brian is the kid in this story and he has been horribly crushed by the same scenario and emotions of the kind in this story and this story describes the way he feels right now and have felt from the very beginning. I hope the IV helper can see how much it hurts Brian for her to have turned against him and shoved him away because of the letter he wrote to her boss, the IV sticker assuming the Director of Speech Pathology was going to turn her against him and put all those ideas in her head about Brian. Brian doesn't even know the man. He never personally met him in his life.

The only time he ever heard from this director was when he made the two phone calls that I originally told you about. He knows nothing about Brian good or bad, he just automatically assumed he was bad just because he asked for a female therapist. But that's what Brian is comfortable with, but the Director of Speech Pathology (a man) didn't understand that. Not only that, he wasn't supposed to call Brian in the first place. He butted in. The outpatient lady therapist was supposed to call me to let me explain him to her first before anything else was done. If he would have, just stayed out of this, this whole thing would have never happened with them or her. Brian just freaked out because of him and he's sorry he did. If this favorite IV helper of Brian's would just call him to let him know everything's okay and that she'll be his nurse again, and mean it and actually be it and be there for him, it would make Brian feel a whole lot better. Then Brian and his favorite IV helper could pretend this whole thing never happened after they worked it out. Then Brian would be happy and never worry about this again. He would be friends with this lady from then on.

I feel like doctors, nurses, and all other hospital staff should be more educated on Autism and on Panic Attacks, because all of the stuff you see happening here is a result of Brian's autism and the fact he had a panic attack when he wrote those letters. Brian was never after anybody. He was just delirious about what people would think of him because of how this director acted and as a result he panicked and wrote all these letters trying to defend himself and beg for mercy at the same time.

Recreation

When Brian and I got married, Brian would sleep all the time except on his days off. Every time he was off we would do something really fun.

We went to Lake Leatherwood every chance we got. It has a walking trail that goes all the way around the lake.

Brian had blessed me with several pair of sandals when we got married. He loved my feet. I always keep my toenails painted so they will be pretty for him. He has a foot fetish! We went to Leatherwood one day. I was wearing one of the pair of sandals he gave me. They had about a one and a half inch heel on them. They were not for trail walking. I managed to ignore how uncomfortable they were about 1/3 of the way around the lake. I had developed major blisters so I went bare foot the rest of the way.

When I was a little girl I went barefoot all the time! I didn't think it would bother me now, but Oh-My! I didn't realize how tender my feet had gotten. As an adult I always were shoes of some kind. I had Brian carry my shoes. A couple of times he gave me a piggy-back ride across some of the really rough parts of the trail. He looks very strong, but he couldn't carry me very far. With Brian you can't read a book by it's cover, he couldn't give me, 115 lbs little girl a ride for long at all.

There was another time we went to Leatherwood, we were almost all the way around the lake. Well, guess what? We saw a snake! Brian is very scared of snakes. This one was a small green grass snake. I told him it wouldn't hurt us. I would scare it with a rock, then we could finish the trail. Oh! No! He wouldn't go that way! It usually took us three hours to walk the whole trail. It was already getting dark. He insisted we turn around, so, we did.

Praise the Lord it was a full moon that night! So, by the time we were almost back we were walking by moonlight. It was so romantic. Brian is so romantic without even trying! We have instances like this one all the time! Not necessarily with a snake but it doesn't matter what we are doing, God enables me to see the romance or humor in every situation we found ourselves in.

It is so awesome how depending on what you choose to focus on in every situation you can be happy or mad. I could have been so angry with him for making me walk 2 ½ more hours that I didn't want to speak to him, because I was so tired. That's impossible because he is so sweet. More importantly, it's wrong according to the Bible. But I chose to focus on all the positives in the situation. Negative is easy to find, if you really try there is always something good to find in your situation. All things work together for the good of those who love the Lord and are called according to his purpose!

I chose to see how it prolonged our time together doing what we love. We both just love to adore God's amazing beauty. We never would have gotten to walk hand in hand by moonlight under the beautiful stars. I wouldn't have ever had the opportunity to pick on him in love for having to do this for a grass snake. Someone told me if it's a pretty snake with a pattern of some kind the snake was poisonous. If the snake was plain or one color, it wasn't. I still don't know if that's true, but I do know that this snake was a grass snake. It would not have hurt anyone. I never would have been able to have this wonderful memory. I am so thankful to God for helping us create this memory I am fond of.

When we went to Leatherwood, we would always camp over night. It was usually Saturday night so we would get ready for Church there. We were able to camp because I volunteered at the New Life

Evangelistic Free Store going through donations. One day a big tent came in and I was able to take it home. We didn't have much money, and, even less now. So, I got a lot of our camping stuff there. Sleeping bags, table cloths, paper towels, etc.

At first, we would gather wood to make a fire to cook on. We went there so much. We got to where we couldn't find any and we had tried charcoal, but we were not patient enough to wait for it to ash over. We were usually so tired and hungry we would be full of chips and dip by the time the burgers and hot dogs would have been done.

When there was no more wood we had to learn to wait, we had no choice.

We always took games. We would play one while waiting to distract us from our hunger. Of course we always had to have Ripple Chips and Cheddar Cheese Dip for my sweet heart when we go camping. He has certain foods he has to have at certain times just like every other Autistic person.

He is not as strict as Raymond on the movie Rain Man. He does, however, have to have cherry turnovers on Sunday. He has to have Ripple Chips and dip when camping. When we first got married it had to be Libby's brand of vegetables. Brian had to have Mr.Pibb to drink and countless other particularities when we first got married. Now it's Pepsi.

I tried to get him to convert to a cheaper brand, but I found out that was NOT going to work. I have the same situation with his Eggo Waffles. I have to but the cheap brand for me, and his kind for him so they will last longer. We only have $120.00 for our groceries each month.

Back to camping. I would set up the tent while Brian walked around chasing the ducks. They were really geese, but he called them ducks. I finally got him to understand if they have a long neck they are geese. This is yet another way Brian is a child. He really thinks if he tries hard enough the geese will let him pet them. He has the innocence of a child.

We were feeding the geese some stale hot dog buns one day and it was time for me to warm our buns on the grill. Well, all the geese were gathered around our grill just waiting for me to lay our buns on the grill. I'm sure they thought, What are you waiting for! Then, Praise the Lord a dog came running down the hill and Brian was able to get a picture of them in mid flight. I know this was of God! Dogs are not allowed in Leatherwood except on a leash!

If it were warm we would swim. Since he is taller than I, I would wrap my legs around his waist and have him go to the really deep part. It was so fun! We would take turns sometimes and hold each other and run. In water you are weightless! We had so much fun!

We had to get 2 huge tarps. We covered the tent with one, put the other one on the floor of the tent before we put anything in it.

If we didn't do this we would wake up wet and cold. We usually camped when the nights were cool so we had to cuddle to stay warm. It was so nice! We would play some games by candle and lantern light before we went to lie down. We were usually exhausted so we would go fast asleep.

When we first got married before we had a tent, we went to every cave around. Brian's favorite cave was Mystic Caverns because he was able to buy a beautiful purple and orange Mystic Caverns T-shirt. Brian really wanted the green shirt and the purple shirt, but we didn't have a lot of money, so we got the green one the first time (green and orange) and went back for the purple t-shirt the next time we went. We've also been to Cosmic Caverns just north of Berryville.

Brian likes the part of the cave where they have the railing around the sides of the inside trail in the cave where the light posts that look like city lights from the 1800s that are on the sides of this trail where the inside lake is located. It's really beautiful there. Before we found Mystic Caverns, this was his favorite cave. We've also been to Hurricane River Cave, and War Eagle Caverns. We went to Onyx once, but we were disappointed when we saw most of the old trails that went deep within the cave were closed. Now, you just go a little ways down and turn left on another trail until you get to the dead end where there's a gate where you turn around. When he was a kid, there were a lot more trails in there to take, and the first trail went further down, deeper into the cave. It's too bad it's not that way now. This was a disappointment to Brian and we haven't been back to that one since.

When we got married Brian would not wear shorts. When the place I volunteered at received some shorts that looked like dress pants with pleats that all changed. I got him one of every color except brown. I got 2 orange pair. I knew that he would like them. He doesn't like boring or plain colors. His clothes have to be bright or green. Not plain green but bright or Christmas green. He also always wore a white t-shirt under all his shirts. The shirts had to button. He will wear bright colored t-shirts or his Mystic Caverns shirt now.

His shirts cannot have any writing on them. I wear a lot of Christian t-shirts, they all have Christian sayings on them. I tried to get him to wear one but he wouldn't, it was white yuck and had writing on it.

However, he will take a T-shirt that has a picture of scenery on it that says something like Eureka Springs, Arkansas, or Mystic Caverns, or Arkansas The Natural State, but these are the only exceptions. Anything else with writing besides this kind of t-shirt he will not wear.

We love to take trails even if we don't really know where we are going. I have to tell you about my favorite experience with walking a trail.

We stopped somewhere just to look. We were not prepared at all.

No water, no cell phone, just the two of us. It was at Point Lookout Trail between Branson and Branson west.

We decided looking at the trail-head map we would only go a little ways around the short loop since it was hot and we had no water or our camera to take pictures with.

Well! This trail was not marked very well. We are talking about two with brain damage and very poor memories. We had to try to remember which way to go.

We started out just fine. It was just beautiful. The trail had several forks in it unmarked so we had no idea which way we were supposed to go in order to take the short .8-mile loop back to the car. We apparently took the wrong one!

We walked for hours! We didn't have any water so every time we to some water on the trail we devoured it. I would say, Look, isn't God good! He is providing us with fresh water! That was a miracle in itself. It not only was hot but very dry.

I remember praying in my heart, Lord, please help us find our way To the car! Satan and his little demons were working overtime just having a ball putting thoughts in my head "Your going to die out here with no water! Nobody knows your even here! Brian doesn't even care, look at him. All the pressure is on you! If you don't get back in time Brian is going to die of dehydration! His mother will never forgive you!

Brian drinks lots of water. As far as him not being bothered by the fact we were lost, he is unable to even experience that kind of fear. Does a child worry about where they are being taken? No! I get the joy of being a wife and a mother.

God is so good! All through my life I never wanted children. I saw first hand how awful the world was and I couldn't rightfully bring a child who I would love into this mess we call life. God knew I would marry one someday, Brian. Wow! My whole life sex equaled love and God protected me from getting pregnant. Isn't that awesome!

Back to the trail we ended up walking the really long loop that went all the way around this huge valley. We walked through this field only to find out it ended at a beautiful river. It was a glorious mess. By the time we got back to our car we decided we had to come back with water, our camera, the cell phone, and we would leave a note on our car with our names and everything!

That's just what we did. You see, a couple of years ago Brian started a hobby. He makes calendars from the pictures we take.

They are absolutely beautiful! He draws by hand the grids, numbers, and days of the week and the month. I have no idea how he came up with the exact measurements to make the grid perfect. I love his calendars. The spaces for each day are plenty big enough to write reminders in. We have at least two in each room. Autistic people fixate on something. Brian's is calendars and this excellent nurse. Even before he made them we always would buy calendars to put in every room.

He really likes making them now because he likes all the pictures in them! Before he would say, I'll be glad when this month is over, I hate the pictures on the calendar. It's too boring. Brian does not like arches, canyons, and deserts. He doesn't like anything to be blue or tan, either. These colors are depressing to him. He mainly likes green, purple, red, and, orange, and the shades thereof. These are his favorite colors. He only likes the green scenery no desert or mountains. Now, that he is able to make his own calendars, he leaves those kind of pictures out. He only uses pictures he likes! He only uses pictures with a lot of greenery. He takes pictures of various places we've been, mostly State Parks in Northwest Arkansas and Southwest Missouri. Some of these places include Lake Leatherwood, the Lost Trail, Withrow Springs, Blue Spring, Roaring River, places on the King's River he likes, and other beautiful locations in between that look very much like the ones I just mentioned.

When I cleaned houses I cleaned in exchange for a nights stay at Dinner Bell Ranch a few times. One time we rode the horses on the trail, I had so much fun! I like to never talked Brian into riding. He insisted on the smallest horse there, even though he weighed 200 pounds.

Brian likes the Lost Trail. His favorite place to camp is usually Lake Leatherwood, but, we have camped at the Lost Trail 5 or 6 times by the bridge that crosses from the parking lot to the campsites. On the other side of this bridge is a trail that takes approximately 2 hours to go to the end and come back to the front again. There is a big waterfall that comes off a tall cliff at the end of this trail and Brian loves this waterfall which is why this is his favorite trail. Brian calls it Niagara Falls the 2nd. Before you get to the end of this trail, there is a big cave, with a smaller waterfall coming out of it and it pours into a natural pool in the front. We went wading in there once and it was nice and cool. The water is a beautiful teal color. Where we picnic and camp is to the left of the bridge right before the start of the trail and this is our favorite place to picnic or camp out when we go there. God either saves this specific campsite for us or nobody likes to camp there because it's right by the trail-head. It amazingly is always open waiting for us no matter when we decide to go camping there or how many people are already camping there. We often go camping on odd days of the week, like Monday or Tuesday. When Brian worked we went on whatever his days off were.

Occasionally, we like to go to Withrow Springs State Park and we usually have a picnic by the small drop off waterfall where they actually have a table and a grill. One time we took my Aunt-in-law down there to show her what it looks like. She had a blast. She doesn't get out much.

We've been to Roaring River about 2 or 3 times. We don't usually go there as often as we do these other places, but we like the trail that goes behind the river where you can look at the trail and even eventually look at open spaces in the trail where you can see the picnic area and the river and the trail all at the same time. One time, we took my daddy to Roaring River a year or two ago. He seemed to like it too. We had a picnic with him there. This last time we just went ourselves and we took pictures of the river, the picnic area, the cabins, the mountains, the rock formations and, the trail itself and we got some really beautiful pictures out of it.

Blue Spring is a botanical gardens park outside of Eureka Springs and has a beautiful teal green river and several beautiful flowers arranged in sections with paths that go around them. We took a lot of pictures here this past year, too. We went to this park about 5 or 6 times since and had a blast.

Every time someone comes over, Brian has to show everyone his calendars. He would like to show them every one of them, but there usually isn't enough time. He picks his favorite one or two when there isn't time to show them all.

Brian already has 13 calendars made for next year, it's only October, right now.

We finally got our hands on a printer that will do 3 calendars before it runs out of ink. Ink is very expensive. People always tell him he should sell them. They also tell him to make the pictures of the months match the season, but that's not Brian. He has his own process due to his Autism. It may not make sense to anybody else but it makes sense to him.

He would have to charge so much for making them. Because of the time and money for ink he puts into making one it's hard when you can buy them for a $1.00 at most any store. His are personalized and they could decide what picture they wanted on each month. People could make them of family for their grandparents. The possibilities are endless. I just don't want his hobby to become work where he has no joy in it anymore. Brian also likes to color in coloring books, but these are no ordinary coloring books, these are complicated coloring books of butterflies, birds, flowers, carousel horses, angel & nativity scenes, etc. that he bought at Silver Dollar City and he mixes the colors to make it exact until it matches the picture on the book cover perfectly. We put 3 of his coloring books in the Berryville Fair and he won 2 red ribbons and 1 blue ribbon for it. We also put 3 of his calendars in the fair and he got blue ribbons on all 3 of them. He also made stain glass carousel horse and they are hanging in the windows in the Family Room, and he got blue ribbons for both of them at the Berryville Fair.

Sometimes we like to go to Silver Dollar City. Our favorite time is during the Christmas season when we get to see the five story Christmas tree lit up. This tree also plays music (Christmas songs) every 15 minutes from 6:00 pm-9:00 pm. This tree plays Carol of the Bells and this is my husband's favorite. I bought him a snow globe of the five story tree and it plays Carol of the Bells and he really likes it. It sounds and looks absolutely beautiful and we really like it. We also like to see the Dickens Christmas Play every time we go in November and December. We sing Christmas carols around a camp fire every night the Passion Play does Beyond Dickens during these months. We have so much fun. We meet people from all over the world. We have made some very good friends there.

For a couple of years they had this really beautiful music in the summer at the Opera House called, For the Glory. We absolutely loved that and went to it every-time we went to Silver Dollar City. Brian likes to look in all the gift shops and see all the crafts, antiques, candy, candles, coloring books, scenic t-shirts, Victorian dresses, lace, quilts, blankets, paintings, etc. This is nice to do in the summer, but it is especially nice to do during the Christmas season because they have all their Christmas stuff out.

Brian will not ride the rides because he is afraid of heights, so we just look in the shops and then eat at concessions and have things like nachos, funnel cakes, chicken, coconut pie, rolls, cornbread, cotton candy, dip-n-dots, etc. These are the things that Brian likes to get, and he usually likes to eat at the Aunt Polly's restaurant to get the chicken, coconut pie, rolls, cornbread, a bag of chips and a coke. He still goes to the other stands some of the time, but this is his favorite place to eat. I usually get either a hot dog or a potato skillet. Brian usually likes to buy the taffy candy bars, too.

Sometimes, during the Christmas season we save up our money ahead of time and buy each other Christmas presents there at the end of the season when they are marked 75% off. We also like to go to the downtown Eureka Springs gift shops on our anniversary, December 22nd. We're usually real happy with what we got when We're done because we can get some really beautiful stuff at all these gift shops really cheap because it's the end of the season. This makes it really nice for us, because we save our quarters all year long to pay for our anniversary suite with a Jacuzzi in it. Any extra money after the room we use for spending money. We already paid our room off in July, so all the quarters we save until our anniversary we'll be able to spend. We never spend any change at all. We have a quarter anniversary bear, and coffee cans, decorated with Christmas paper for nickels, dimes, and, pennies. We also have a large coffee can decorated in Christmas paper for our $1 bills. I'm usually the only one who puts dollars in there, but I'm glad because it's always there when we need it to go have fun on.

Occasionally, we like to go bowling at the Town& Country lanes, but we don't go real often because it costs too much money. Brian bought me my very own bowling ball a few years ago. It is absolutely beautiful. It's very colorful, green, red and yellow!

Sometimes we'll play pool when we visit Brian's uncle at his house. He has a pool table in his basement. We played with his cousin once who Brian thought he'd never beat because his cousin is really good. But Brian finally beat him once or twice. Brian felt like that was a big accomplishment. We also played darts with this same cousin, and this cousin started out beating him, but he made a comeback with this, too. We have a dartboard at our house. So when Brian's in the mood, sometimes we'll play it at our house.

Brian likes to play miniature golf every once in a while, so, since we have a 3-park pass for Silver Dollar City, Celebration City, and White Water we usually play at Celebration City for $1.00. About the only other fun thing we do there is ride the carousel. The rest of the time we go in the shops and concession stands because Brian won't ride any of the rides because he's afraid of heights.

We recently went to Abilene Texas to see his mother, she has Breast Cancer. While we were there Brian took me on our first real date in his home town. We ate the most wonderful burgers I have ever eaten at Whataburger. Then he took me to a mini golf place to play golf and play Skeeball. I had so much fun! It was really neat to have a husband who wanted to take you all over town to show you off to everyone he could find.

We like to play skeeball sometimes. When we do, we usually go to Fun Spot to play it for a quarter a game. When we get a lot of tickets we turn them in for prizes.

Brian has spells where he likes to play the piano and practice on it, but he'll usually keep it up a month or two and then give up for several months before he gets the urge to play again. When we first got married we bought several things that we could not pay for out right like our piano. We would just pay five or ten dollars when we could till we paid whatever it was off. We have never had or ever will have a credit card. We have very good credit with everyone in our home town and neighboring towns because of this.

We like going on scenic drives and looking at all the pretty trees. This is a lot of fun. We don't get to do this as often now that car gas is so much higher.

We like to go eat out a lot. We usually go to Pizza Hut, Kentucky Fried Chicken, Taco Bell, Subway, Pancake House, Dos Rios, and, Good times Pizza. We use our recreation money for this. We have an envelope budget. We budget $100 for our recreation, when it's gone it's gone unless we have one dollar bills in our one dollar can.

Sometimes we like to have friends over to eat and have tacos, or spaghetti. One time we had beef ramen noodle, but we don't usually make that for guests. Sometimes we'll have pot roast and invite a family over from church that we like, and we eat and talk about various things and Brian usually likes to show off his calendars when someone comes over and give them a tour of the house.

The rest of the time Brian likes to go visit relatives off and on.

We've also been going to the Eureka Springs Nursing Home to visit the patients. We originally went there because the mother of the eye doctor's wife I cleaned house for was in there for the last few months of her life. I was very close to her. When she lived at her home 6 blocks from our house, I used to go to her house every morning and sing every hymn that I knew by heart out of our church hymnal after I retired from cleaning houses. I took the hymnal I used to sing out of to the nursing home. I wrote in the front cover for Big Bertha to sing to Momma Esther. Now almost every time we go to the nursing home I sing out of it The patients just love it. I sing silly on certain songs just to make them laugh.

Our Home

When Brian moved into our little mansion November 25th, he had everything we would ever need! What we didn't have from his hope chest the ex-owner left for us. We made monthly payment of $50 till we paid all $900. He gave us a really good deal! It was of God! This price included a real nice Maytag washer and dryer set, a Kitchen Aid side by side refrigerator with an ice and chilled water dispenser in the door of the freezer, a King size bed, a Queen size headboard with 2 matching end tables, a clothes hutch and a huge dresser with a mirror and shelves, A Lawn Man mower, a computer with a desk, a gas stove and a back porch full of antique lanterns! On top of this he gave us his kitchen table with 4 cushioned chairs, and a record player stand 3 feet tall with glass.

When we got the house it had blue and pink wallpaper in the living room and blue carpet. 2 toned blue cabinets in the kitchen and a 2 toned blue bathroom. The toilet was even blue. I have a feeling their favorite color was blue! The kitchen was peach colored. The office was a lighter peach. One of the bedrooms was what I call Hello Yellow, it was like a room of pure sun. The other bedroom was a mint green.

The outside was brick red colored paint with peach shutters that had arrow shaped holes on each side.

Boy oh boy does it ever look different now. The built in garage which had concrete floors, with a little room in the back that used to be a bathroom is now carpeted in green of course, jasper green.

We converted the old bathroom to where we keep our stand up freezer. We got the freezer free at the furniture bank in town. It was so neat. We went there because everything is free and we didn't have any extra money to buy any of the few things we still needed like a couch. God is good! We got there at the exact time. Someone was bringing a freezer to be unloaded. I saw it, asked if it worked, it did. I asked the driver if instead of unloading it there if he would just take it to my house. I had already talked to the furniture bank people. I told them we only had a Mercury Topaz and we would have no way of hauling it. He said, Sure. I'm sure he was thinking, I hope it's not far. It was only about blocks to our house.

He and Brian put it in our ugly garage. It had long nails sticking out of this grayish paneling with holes busted in it everywhere. Now it's beautiful! I plucked all the nails out and covered all the wholes with duck tape. If you can't fix it, duck it! That's my hillbilly philosophy. Then, we painted the ugly panel's confetti fanfare peach. We also have a grandfather clock in there and a beautiful chandelier. Picture of chandelier

Brian fell in love with the chandelier when we went to an antique shop in town He just had to have it. It costs three hundred dollars. We paid it out like we have all the other beautiful stuff we now own. People don't need credit cards, we have never had one, nor will we ever get one. Thanks to our good reputation of paying our debts, there's no need for one. We also have an antique hutch teal green of course, a beautiful dining set with a buffet, a table with Christmas striped padded chairs, and, the matching hutch that we have in our kitchen.

I have Christmas vinyl table cloths on both tables. We have Christmas decorations, wreaths, arrangements, etc., most of which I made myself. I absolutely love crafts. There are 2 bookcases that a really good friend of ours gave us, and a greenish blue cabinet full of games.

We love to play games! We have almost every traditional game ever made. We could play games for hours, it beats watching the trash on Television now a days. We don't have cable, just an antenna. We usually watch VCR tapes of Feature Films for Families or something Christian. We do however have a few worldly tapes like Hope Floats, While you were sleeping, and, the classic, Titanic.

As far as the other rooms in the house go we have a purple bedroom which is either lilac or lavender and pretty pictures on the wall like the waterfall poster we have hanging on the wall, a picture of a lady that looks like she might be an angel, and, one other painting and 3 calendars.

We also have a cheap antique lamp that sits on our dresser next to the TV and it has roses painted on it. The carpet in this room is a peach blossom color. For our guest room we have a green bedroom (mint green) and a dresser with antique trinkets we got from Dollar General, plus a brush and mirror set we got at an antique shop. We have a chest of drawers, with an antique looking green clock we got at Dollar General and two or three other trinkets. Above this in the corner are two paintings. One of a snow scene and the other a summer scene picture that we bought at Silver Dollar City. We also have several other pretty pictures on the wall with flowers and cats and other things. The carpet is a peach blossom color. Our office was a pink peach originally and we repainted it a pumpkin peach color. We have a big summer scene picture with a lake, a barn, and, a mountain in it in the center of the wall. To the left of this we have a red Merry Christmas sign with green leaves. To the right of this we have a picture of us taken around Christmas time about two years ago. To the right of that we have a calendar. On the sidewall we have a record player in front of the window we play Christmas music on. To the right of it a shelf case with books and tapes. On the opposite wall another calendar and then an open entryway with Christmas garland over the top of it and a green Merry Christmas sign. After that, on the other side wall a closet, and then an open wall with a shelf case at the end of it, which has a calendar on it. The carpet is Teal Feather green.

In the living room we have a velvet red wall with a gold mirror in the center of it and two gold hanging things on each side of it. Under it an entertainment center with a TV in it and garland and Christmas lights around the edges and around the shelves it has. We have a nativity scene on the top of it, and, trinkets on the shelves. To the left a tall Christmas tree we keep up all year. To the right of this an antique green couch with an end table at the other end of it and in front of the entry way an antique green matching chair. On the other sidewall is another couch we simply covered with red curtains to make it look like Christmas and a coffee table in front of it and an end table beside it. We have a Christmas town set up on the bottom shelf. And the top of this table is glass so you can see it. The carpet in there is teal feather green.

In the kitchen, the walls are apple red (I call it Shicken Red) and the cabinets are two tones of green, a pine green trim and a lighter mint-like green color (not the same as the green bedroom but similar).

In the bathroom the walls are painted spearmint green with teal green borders. There is also a corner cabinet painted teal green and a waterfall picture to the side of it. There is also a shelf case full of trinkets between that wall and the bathtub with another picture above it. Above the toilet is the towel rack with green and red towels and above that is a picture of three angels with instruments.

In the hallway we have sea green shelves with cards, trinkets, and stuffed animals. The top 3 shelves are stuffed animals that Brian got me. They are so adorable. On the bottom 3 shelves are full of beautiful Christmas cards, trinkets, and, snow globes. Brian collects these items. I haven't got him any of these for Christmas lately because were out of room.

I got convicted one day, and, went through all our tapes. I got rid of anything rated about PG13. I even got rid of some of those. As for all the games, I already had a lot of them. I've always loved games. Brian's favorite was Parcheesi for a while, I can't even tell you how many times we've played that one. Now, his favorite board game is Titanic. In the game Titanic you have to advance from 2nd class to 1st class by landing on the 5 locations that give you a card, that would be a Passport card, the Key to the Room, the Valuables card you get when you land in your room, the Health Check (Infirmary) Card, and, a Life Vest. Then, when you make it to First Class you have to try to get to the lifeboat before anyone else and the one that makes it to the lifeboat first wins. It's kind of like the game Clue and the game Parcheesi put together, but in this game instead of getting out of jail and going home, you go from class to class and try to get to the lifeboat before anybody else, and, if you do, you win. We have a little game we play every time he chooses to play one of these two games I say Oh no. Again?! smiling the whole time Two other games we play a lot are Yahtzee and Rummy, although, we still play the other 20 or 30 games we have, but these are the ones we play the most.

Autistic Traits

Right now, Brian is a high functioning autistic individual, but this was not always the case. He developed way slower than other people his age as a baby and even as a child. It took him several years to catch up. He spoke in phrases for a long time and couldn't even carry on a normal conversation until the seventh grade, age 13 ½ to 14 ¼ years. When he was in Elementary School and especially when he was a baby, if someone even suggested he might go to college one day people would have thought they were nuts. Back then, people said, he's never going to make it. There's no way he'd ever make it that far. He's too bad off. He doesn't stand a chance. We'll be lucky if he even makes it at all. I will talk about this more in another book I'm writing about Brian's infancy and childhood. After I tell you how bad off he was then you will be absolutely shocked he made it this far.

Back then there was no way he'd ever stand a chance, but he finally caught up with everybody else by about his 3rd year of college. He is shockingly far more intelligent now than he was when he was a child. Now however, he's in a predicament where he feels like he might as well not have made it, because yes, he's intelligent, but he can't get what's in his head out his hands or out his mouth, and it is very frustrating for him. There will be times when he has a blank look on his face and I'll know what he wants to say. I'll say it for him. People have come to me asking me if I didn't think anything Brian said was important because they have noticed I never let him finish what he's trying to say. I explain, I know what he's thinking. I also know what it is he wants to say, but he just can't, so I say it for him. I asked him after several people have told me this if he minded me doing that and he said, No. I'm glad you do it, because you always say what I'm wanting to say, but I can't. I can't believe he didn't say yes! He will answer, yes to most any question. I really have fun with this. I'll say, "You hate me don't you." He almost always says yes, sometimes he'll catch on and not fall for my trick. I don't get all my attention when he catches me. When he falls for it I pout and milk it for all it's worth! His social and emotional intelligence is badly lacking, and his performance ability on a job is very shaky. When Brian tried to work right after we got married it took him forever to learn his job. Now, when he finally knew what to do, it only lasted a little while. During that time, you couldn't ask for a better worker. One day, out of the blue he would go to work and not have any idea what he was supposed to do. Sequencing is extremely hard for Brian. Things that make sense to you and me doesn't make since to Brian. They do not fit into the way things should be according to his autistic world.

I just wanted you to know he hasn't been exactly the same as most autistics because most high functioning autistics were always high functioning. Not him, he was low functioning, and after several years of being educated to death, his mother drilled him constantly. She wanted him to have a normal life. Now he is finally high functioning, but his intelligence is of no use to him because it doesn't help him to perform like everyone else does on a job. I'd like you to see some of the autistic tendencies he has now to show you what he is like as an adult, and how his autism affects him. Some of these have already been covered, but I'd like to show you a few more of his tendencies that I haven't covered yet. So, here it goes.

Being autistic Brian does not like change. I thought the home was the wife's territory to do with as she pleased. Not with an autistic husband. I found out the hard way.

One day my cousin-in-law came over to our house to help me decorate a little. She wanted to switch the couch and the entertainment center with each other. NOT! Brian got very upset! He was very set on keeping it the same. She was helping me hang wallpaper in our living room. Red my favorite color! When we finished we started to put the stuff back differently. Brian walked into the room. That was not a good thing! He demanded that everything be put back the exact way it was.

I now know I need to okay every change I make with him. I have gotten to make a few changes. I was able to talk him into just trying it for a few days. Even then I sometimes have to put it back because it doesn't sit well with him. This isn't a bad thing. In fact it helps our relationship for me to find out by trial and error what he likes. He is unable to flat out tell you what he likes or doesn't, you have to search for it. It's like being on an adventure all the time. Life is far from ever plain with him around.

We decorated our house the way he wanted it. I didn't really have a say in how it was done. This would bother most women. Not me, I love his way of doing things. I don't think I would have had the nerve to decorate my house in Christmas all year long without a really good excuse. Because of how depressed my husband was when it came time to take all the decorations down. I had to leave them up. It broke my heart to see him that way!

Our house is painted all Christmas colors. Our carpet is two kinds of green. The living room, hallway, and office are teal green. The family room (built in garage) is jasper green.

Brian is afraid of the dark. Before we got married he kept every light in the house on when he was at home. When he was a child he was afraid of the bushes. He was afraid there was something behind them where he couldn't see. Even after we got married I would constantly have to follow him turning off the lights. Still do!

He has a severe fear of storms. Thank God our house had a storm cellar when he bought it. The first two years of our marriage we spent many nights cuddled together on a one-person cot that his mother gave us. If the town storm alarm went off ever if it was a severe thunderstorm he insisted we go to the cellar. I finally got him to understand that our heavenly father will take care of us during a thunderstorm. Now if it is a tornado storm we still go down there, rightfully so. God gave us brains we should use them.

He is deathly afraid of knives too. When we have a watermelon I have to cut it because he is too afraid of cutting himself. You should see the look of fear on his face even if I just pick one up and he sees it.

He is also afraid of razors. He refused to use one. He has to have an electric razor. I had to shave him once for an operation once. I thought he was going to have a heart attack!

Talk about a picky eater! I've read how some autistic people don't like certain foods because of its texture. Brian doesn't like some foods because they are not the brand he likes. Soup has to be Campbell's. Chili has to be Hormel NO BEANS! He also likes his hotdogs to be skinny, all beef hotdogs, usually Oscar Myers. He doesn't like his foods mixed, either, and he doesn't like casserole. He'll only eat a few vegetables, too. The rest he doesn't like the taste of. He likes corn, peas, and green beans canned if it's Libby's.

Brian usually doesn't like off brands of any kind. He does like carrots, celery, and baked potatoes, but that's about it for vegetables. If it's good for Brian chances are he's not going to like it. On the other hand, he loves any kind of junk food, chips, homemade cookies, soda pop, candy, and homemade cakes. He absolutely cannot stand pre-made cakes from the store. He says they are spongy. He likes crumbly cake dough, not spongy! He loves it when I make him a cake. When we first got married it had to be Milk Chocolate but they no longer make the original milk chocolate, it's Dutch milk chocolate. He decided he could eat German Chocolate. It's the closest thing I could find that looked like milk chocolate on the box. Brian is very picky about what the food looks like on the can or the box. It doesn't matter to him if it has the very same ingredients. If the box is different he doesn't like it.

Brian has unusual skills in some areas, but is pretty poor at everything else. He can pronounce and spell long medical words that may have up to 20 or 30 letters in them. He can usually spell or pronounce these words on the first try, but when he doesn't, he usually figures it out in 2 or 3 tries. He can hear tunes that are theme songs to shows on the TV and be able to pick out the notes on the piano with his right hand and make it sound just like what he just heard. For some reason though, he can't do this with his left hand, When he tries to play music that's written he has difficulty getting his left hand to cooperate with his right hand, he fumbles all over the place because of it. When he took Anatomy & Physiology at a Technical College he had the terms down like a steel trap, but when he took a clinical class that required laboratory experiments where he had to use this knowledge to perform a task he was totally lost. He takes really good pictures with a camera and after some of the pictures he took this year, he's decided he must have a talent with photography. Most people feel the same way that he has shown his pictures to, mainly his calendars. What's funny though, he'll have several fuzzy pictures in one batch of pictures and turn right around after taking about 300 pictures and have about 10 or 20 really good ones. He can sing very well, but with music theory classes where he has to rewrite tough pieces that use techniques that professionals used to make a music composition he is totally lost. And, no, he cannot play another instrument well enough to be able to do both like the record companies out there would like him to be able to do. He only has the talent with the voice. His piano playing ability is only on the level of an intermediate.

That's as far as he's ever able to get and still play well, if he ever does master a hard piece, he has to start all over again if he does another one and it takes just as long to get it down as it did the first one, which is a long time. Some people think that because he is able to do these few things that he ought to be able to do many other things well, but this is simply not the case. He is limited to these few things. Also he does well at academics, but when it comes to performing a job he's pretty much shot, especially at manual labor jobs.

Sometimes Brian does not always know how to socialize in a group setting, so when he's unsure of himself he may not say much of anything because he feels overwhelmed.

As you can probably already see from reading this, sometimes Brian can do something very complicated and then not get it when it comes to something simple.

There are times when Brian has difficulty expressing his needs. Sometimes he tries to explain things in writing, but he occasionally gets in trouble for this because some people don't understand.

Brian also learns things by repetition.

Brian is also easily panicked when people treat him like the director treated him that I told you about. He's very vulnerable and this gets him all shook up.

Brian does not like the things that most men like. He is not mechanically inclined and does not like auto mechanics, sports, fishing, hunting. His likes are more similar to that of a girl's.

He likes things like flowers, trinkets, quilts, candy, and candles, all kinds of pretty stuff you would find in gift shops. So, if you get him something for Christmas such as a pocketknife or tools he will be very depressed. Someone actually bought him a pocketknife for Christmas once and he went back and traded it in for a watch. This made the person that gave him the gift very disappointed in him.

Sometimes he gets a blank look on his face when you tell him something and you'll figure out by looking at him that he probably didn't get it. Sometimes Jumpstart 1st Grade he catches things just fine, but other times he doesn't get it at all.

It is a true joy to be married to Brian! I pray everybody could have as wonderfully sweet a man as I do! It takes all kinds to make up the world we live in.

If you have any questions or comments about my book feel free to contact me at 1-(870) 423-6112. I would love to hear from you, I'm sure Brian would too. He has been such a help to me. He has a much better memory than I do plus he can spell. I really frustrated him because I'm so slow typing. He can type 40 words a minute! I type maybe 10 words a minute!

Top picture: Brian's Granny's house.
Bottom one: Brian's painting of the same house.

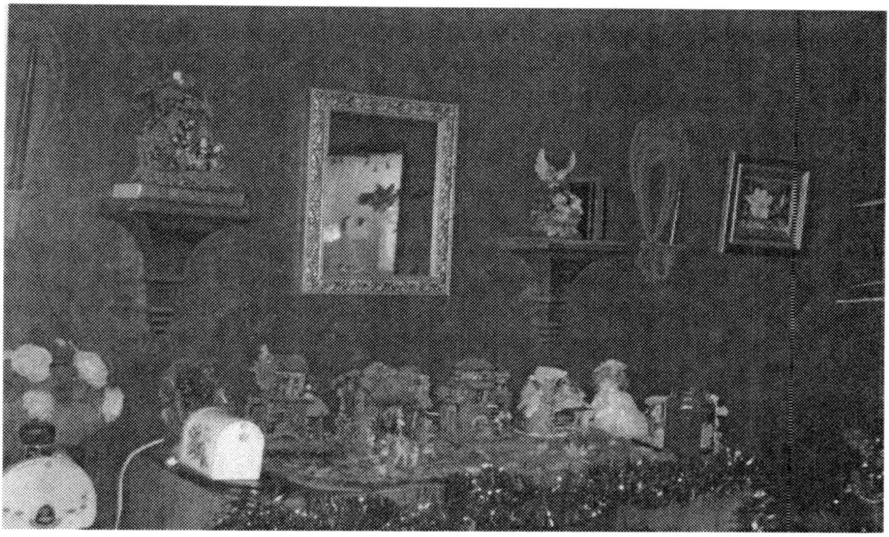

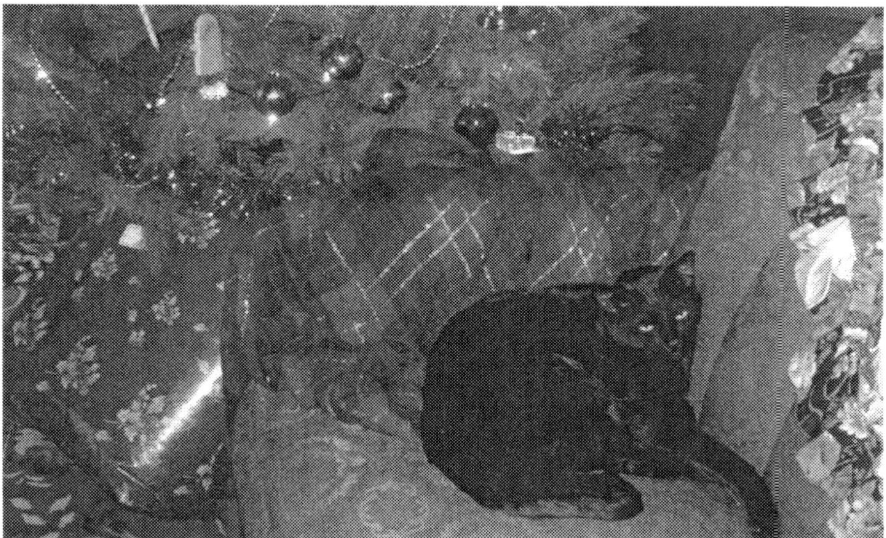

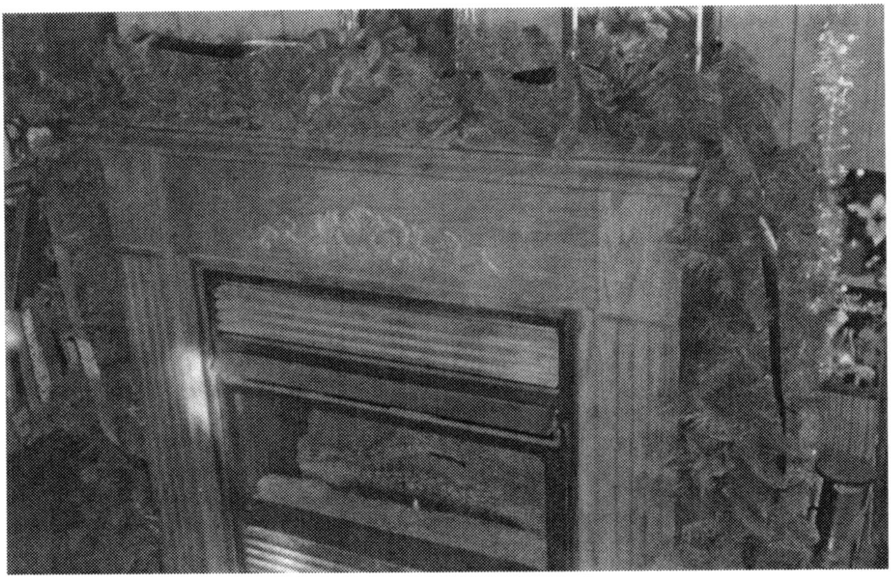

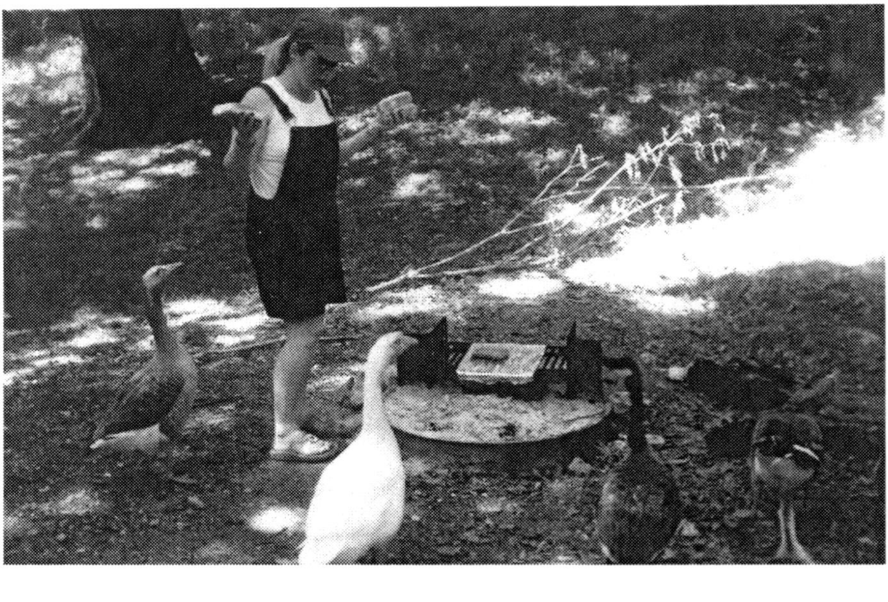

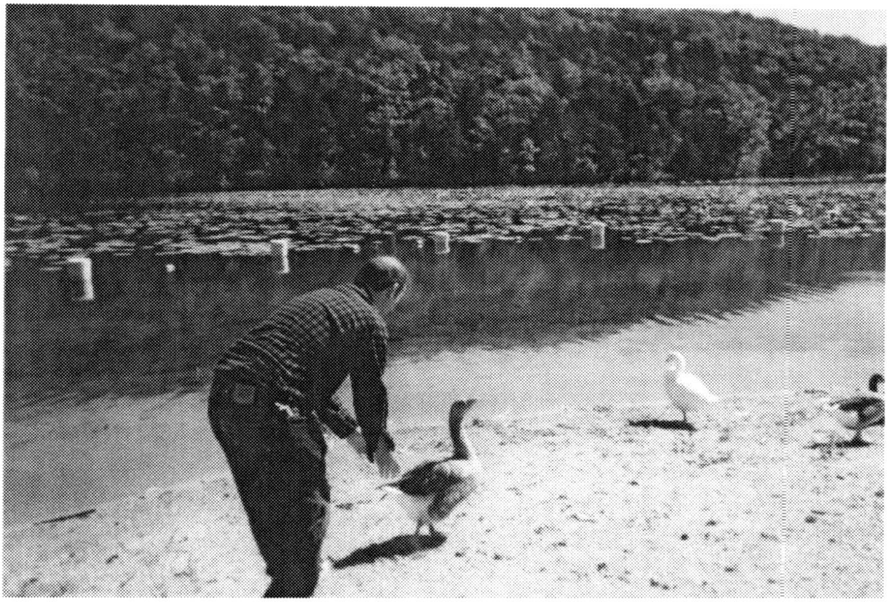

Printed in the United Kingdom
by Lightning Source UK Ltd.
131759UK00002B/40/A